THE MOTORMAN
AND HIS DUTIES

A Handbook of Theory and Practice for
Operating Electric Cars

BY
LUDWIG GUTMANN
CONSULTING ELECTRICAL ENGINEER

FIFTH EDITION REVISED AND ENLARGED
BY
GEORGE RICHMOND METCALFE, M. E.

CHICAGO
WINDSOR & KENFIELD PUBLISHING CO.
1903

©2006-2010 PERISCOPE FILM LLC
ALL RIGHTS RESERVED
ISBN #978-1-935700-06-7
WWW.PERISCOPEFILM.COM

COPYRIGHT 1898
BY WINDSOR & KENFIELD PUBLISHING CO.

COPYRIGHT 1903
BY WINDSOR & KENFIELD PUBLISHING CO.

©2006-2010 PERISCOPE FILM LLC
ALL RIGHTS RESERVED
ISBN #978-1-935700-06-7
WWW.PERISCOPEFILM.COM

INTRODUCTION.

The purpose of this work is to so familiarize the reader with the operation of an electric car, that the practical duties of a motorman may be the more easily and quickly learned. At the same time it will be found to explain, in simple language devoid of mathematics and technicalities, many points not generally understood by the average motorman, and a knowledge of which cannot fail to make his services more valuable to his company and satisfactory to himself; and also to better fit him for promotion.

The motorman who understands his business is able to operate the cars that are put in his charge with much less danger of accident, and with less power and less wear on the equipment, than a man who simply knows how to get his car over the road on time. This book is not only intended to explain the electrical part of an electric motor car, but to give some general instruction and advice to those who desire to make this work their livelihood. It is based on the experience gathered for a number of years in the electric railway field, instructing motormen in their duties and work, and on results and observations made on roads in practical life. To explain some electrical effects it has been necessary to adopt a few comparisons, which, while not exactly correct from a scientific standpoint, give the reader a clear picture of what is meant.

By closely reading this book and following the advice given the reader should be able to acquire a responsible vocation in a comparatively short time, and he has the assurance that he does not drop into it in a haphazard fashion, but has a guide to lead him over a road yet unknown to him, a road which is made considerably shorter and smoother by this method than learning entirely from experience.

In securing illustrations and collecting data for describing the electric machines and devices, the author desires to acknowledge the generous assistance of the manufacturing companies whose apparatus is explained in the following pages.

This work is divided into two parts. Part I. treats of the practical work of a motorman. Part II. will be found to explain more in detail the theory and construction of the apparatus.

THE AUTHOR.

CHAPTER I.

A GLANCE OVER THE CAR EQUIPMENT.

A man who will read and study as well as gain from practical experience will be worth a great deal more than the average motorman of today, and he should be able to secure a position more readily. Experience has shown that a motorman who is familiar with the track, switches and curves and who has been in the employ of the company for some time can operate a car with a very much smaller current consumption than a new man. It is the same comparison of an experienced and inexperienced fireman in the boiler room. It is evident that the more a man knows about his vocation the better compensation he can expect. A man may start as a motorman and by faithful service and study he may advance to be a car inspector, line inspector and eventually electrician of the road.

A man wishing to qualify himself for a motorman can advance in two ways: by experience in operating a car and by studying the theory of the electrical equipment. For rapid advancement the practical work should be accompanied by electrical reading.

The reader who wishes to become proficient and know more than just simply enough to run his car over the road, should be of a practical and mechanical turn of mind. He should know something about the use of tools and machinery. To become familiar with the electric car equipment the best plan is to work at first in the barns and repair shops. One will there learn the practical side. He will

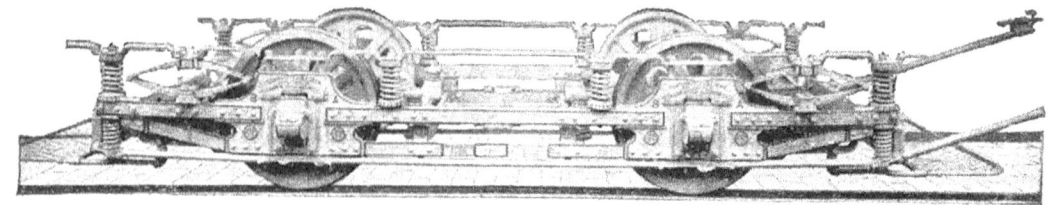

FIG. 1.

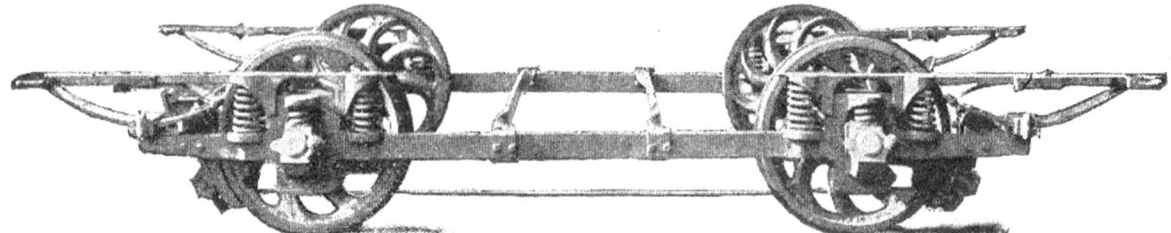

FIG. 2.

FIG. 3.

FIG. 4.

have to mount motors on trucks or repair defective pieces of machinery, and by frequently handling them he will soon familiarize himself with their names and uses. However, not everyone can have such preparation for a position as motorman, and for this reason we will do the next best thing, namely, take an imaginary trip through the car shop and mention briefly the various parts of an electric car equipment and the devices that are necessary to operate it. Then these devices will be described in detail further on and the principles on which they work will be explained.

To begin with, we see trolley wires entering the repair shop and cars brought in and taken out. Now, there are many persons who have seen this done, but few understand the operation in its details and the many devices and appliances that are necessary to accomplish it.

The electric current as it flows in the wires is invisible, and although they look "dead" to us they may be transmitting hundreds of horse power of energy. It is necessary to be cautious about coming in contact with suspended wires and nothing should be touched that may be connected in any way with a circuit or a severe shock will be received.

A motor car is composed of the following essential parts:

1. A car body for carrying the passengers.
2. A car truck and wheels for carrying the motors and car body.
3. Motors for propelling the car.
4. A trolley for taking the power from the overhead wire.
5. Controllers for admitting current to the motor windings and regulating the amount of power conducted to the motors.
6. Brakes for stopping the car.
7. Devices for protecting the motors, such as fuses, lightning arresters and switches.

Figs. 1 to 4 show different constructions of car trucks, but these are only a few of the types which are in general use.

FIG. 5.

Figs. 1 and 2 show different styles of single trucks which are used on short cars of from 25 to 30 ft. in length. Figs. 3 and 4 show bogie trucks which are used with long cars, two

FIG. 6.

such trucks being used under each car. The essential parts of all street car trucks consist of two sets of wheels mounted on axles which are held in position by bearings. The bearings are fixed to the side frames which give the truck its rigidity. Springs are placed between the bearings and the parts on which the car body rests in order to prevent too severe jarring of the car body. In the case of the single trucks the lower sills of the car are bolted directly to the side frames of the truck, but where double trucks are used a piece known as the truck bolster extends between the two side

FIG. 7

frames and is pivoted at its center to the car body bolster. The brake rigging is also a very important part of the equipment of the truck, and on most modern electric cars both hand and power brakes are used. The brakes and brake rods are shown on the trucks illustrated, and are of a number of different patterns, some of which will be described in a later chapter. The location of the brake shoes is normally from $\frac{1}{8}$ to $\frac{1}{4}$ in. distant from the wheels. Fig. 5 shows a car mounted upon a single truck and Fig. 6 shows a double truck car.

An electric railway motor mounted on an axle between the car wheels is shown in Fig. 7. The wheels and axle have been taken from underneath the truck. The motor consists of two principal parts; the outer case, which is called the field magnet and which is stationary, and an inner rotating part called the armature. The electric motor and the principles governing it will be explained in a subsequent

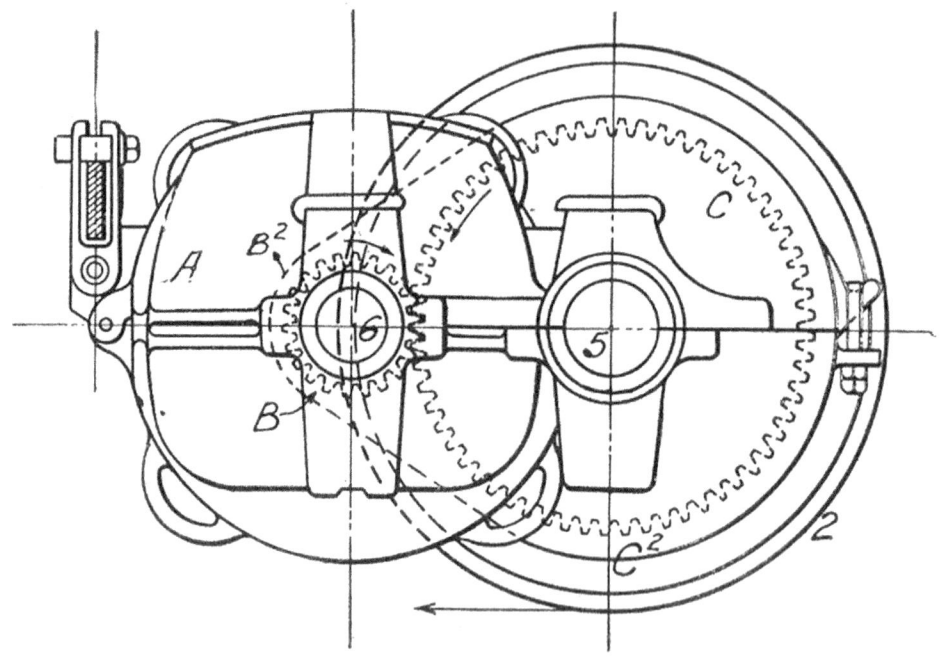

FIG. 8.

chapter. Figs. 7 and 8 give a general idea of the appearance of the motor and may be referred to together. On one end of the armature shaft 6 is keyed a pinion B as shown in Fig. 8, but in service the pinion and the gear into which it meshes are covered by a casting as B^1 C^1 in Fig. 7. This pinion meshes with a split gear which is fastened on the car axle. The car axle passes through the bearing 5 as shown in Fig. 9.

Fig. 10 shows one form of split gear which is mounted on the car axle and engages with the pinion B. The manner in which the car is propelled will now be made clear. In starting the car a current is sent into the motor which causes the armature to revolve and with it the pinion B. This pinion meshes with the teeth of the split gear C and turns it in a direction opposite to which the pinion rotates. (See Fig.

FIG. 9.

8.) As the pinion B is much smaller in diameter than the split gear C, the car axle to which C is rigidly attached makes a less number of revolutions than does the pinion which drives it. In this way the power developed in the motor is transmitted through the gears to the car axle and the speed of the latter is much less than that of the motor armature. We will now continue to discuss the essential parts of a car equipment, and after we have gone through the repair shop in this way we will take up in the subsequent chapters the theory of these devices and parts, and explain their construction and functions.

Returning to Fig. 8, if the power admitted to the motor turns the armature shaft 6 and pinion B in the direction indicated by the arrow, then the gear C will revolve in the op-

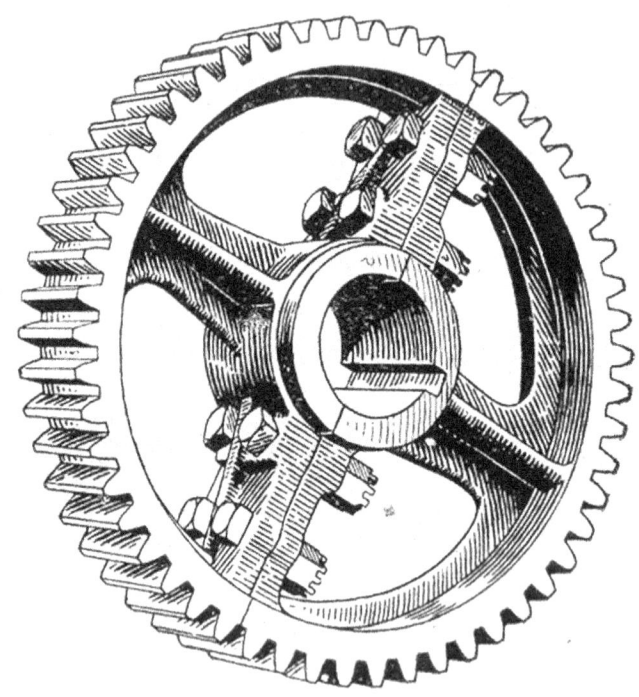

FIG. 10.

posite direction and the car wheel 2 will move from right to left as indicated by the arrow. The functions of the casing B^1 is to protect the pinion and gear wheel from dirt and mechanical injury and if filled with a heavy grease the gears are thus lubricated and preserved and at the same time the noise which they make in running is by this means greatly reduced. In all of the motors illustrated a lid will be noticed over the commutator end of the frame where the brushes are located. These lids are readily removed and their object is to facilitate inspection of the commutator and brushes. Other lids cover holes usually provided for supplying oil to the bearing surfaces. It will be noticed that all of the motors illustrated have their field magnets designed so as to entirely enclose the interior parts, and all the joints of the outer frame are made tight enough to be practically water

FIG. 11.

proof. Water and dirt would readily be thrown into the motor from the car wheels if the parts were not tightly enclosed, but by having the motor cased the windings are protected from water which would cause them to rapidly burn out.

Figs. 11 and 12 show two views of a street car motor with the frame dropped. Fig. 11 shows the lower frame of the motor. dropped leaving the armature in position. The method of dividing field magnets horizontally through the bearings and fastening the lower part at one side by means of hinges is the most usual arrangement for providing for the inspection and repairs of the interior parts of the motor.

FIG. 12.

Fig. 12 shows the lower frame dropped and with it the armature which is ready for removal.

In suspending motors upon car trucks one side of the motor is always held in position by the bearings upon the car axle. The other side of the motor is not fastened rigidly to the frame of the truck, but has springs placed at some point between the motor and the frame in order to avoid the sudden jar which would be occasioned in starting the motor if it were rigidly connected. These springs also serve to

FIG. 13.

greatly increase the life of the gear wheels as part of the shock in starting is taken up by these springs, without which the teeth would be liable to be stripped from the gears. Figs. 13, 14 and 15 represent the same motor with different

FIG. 14.

styles of suspension. Fig. 13 shows what is called the cradle suspension which consists of an iron bar resting on powerful springs which in turn rest on the truck. This method is designed to relieve the motor bearings of the weight of the motor, which being suspended in the line of its center of gravity is supported without undue strains.

FIG. 15.

Fig. 14 shows the parallel bar suspension and Fig. 15 the nose suspension. The latter is the one most commonly used.

FIG. 16.

A type of motor differing in some respects to those previously illustrated is shown in Fig. 16. This is known as the box frame type and it differs from the split frame type in that the magnet frame is cast in practically one piece forming a cube with well rounded corners and large openings at each end into which the frames carrying the bearings for the armature shaft are bolted. The armature is put in place or removed through these end openings in the frame. Motors of this type are mounted or moved from the truck by means of a crane from above when the truck is out from under the cars, and no track pit is required. In order to

FIG. 17.

facilitate removing the armatures from these motors a special tool is provided, shown in Fig. 17, upon which the motor is mounted. The armature shaft is centered on this tool and by removing the bolts from one of the frame heads and moving the motor frome to one end of the tool by means of the hand wheel, the armature is left entirely exposed and mounted upon centers where it may be readily inspected or repaired.

Fig. 18 is a diagram of the wiring in a car. The two controllers are represented at the extreme ends and the four

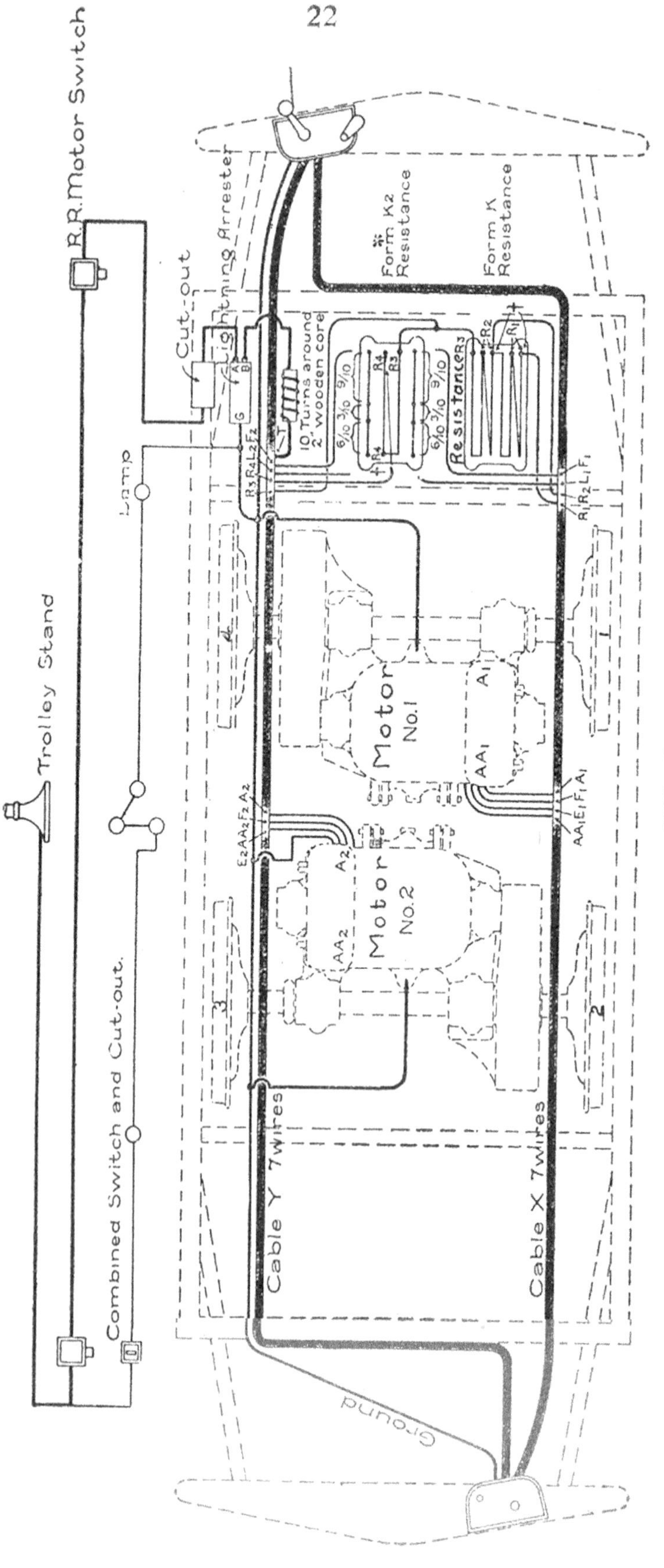
R.R. Motor Switch
Trolley Stand
Combined Switch and Cut-out
Lamp
Cut-out
Lightning Arrester
Form K2 Resistance
Form K Resistance
10 Turns around 2" wooden core
Resistances
Motor No.1
Motor No.2
Cable Y 7 wires
Cable X 7 wires
Ground

FIG. 18.

car wheels are indicated by 1, 2, 3 and 4; between these four wheels are shown the outlines of the two motors. Heavy tube-like connection from the controllers to the motors represents a hose which surrounds the wires going to each motor. It protects them partly from mechanical injury and partly from dampness, and water thrown by wheels or rails. The box marked "resistance" is used in starting the car and will be explained in the chapter on controllers. The resistance, hose and other devices are beneath the car floor. One wire entering the hose comes from the trolley. This wire

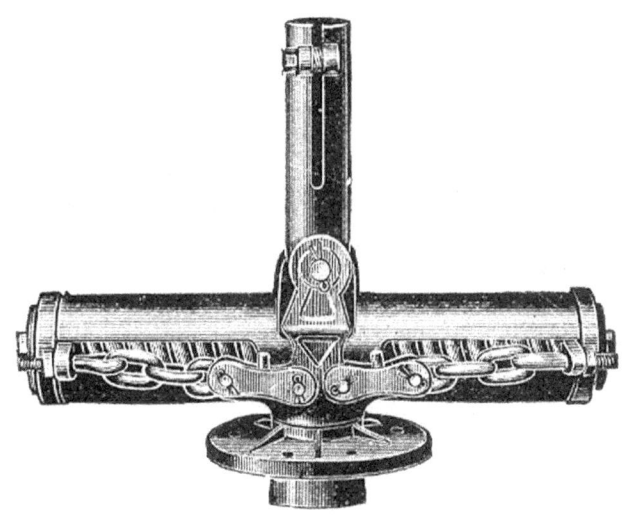

FIG. 19.

is led from the roof of the car down the corner post and passes through the lightning arrester and fuse box.

There are many styles of trolley bases. In Figs. 19 and 20 two forms are shown. The trolley wire is generally attached to the iron base below a screw provided with one or two washers. The springs are employed for the purpose of causing an upward pressure on the trolley pole, which is not shown. The pole can be removed from the trolley base and is held adjustably in a socket. A great range of movement is necessary in the springs and trolley pole as the trolley wire (the wire suspended in the air) cannot be attached at the same height over all the course of travel. For instance, at railroad crossings it is placed much higher so as not to interfere with the railroad service and brakemen who may be standing on the roofs of the cars; again it may be much lower in other places, such as bridges and tunnels. The trolley pole is a long iron or wooden pole on the end of which is located the "trolley." This trolley, which consists of brass or gun metal, is generally a small, narrow wheel with projecting flanges, though some European roads use a

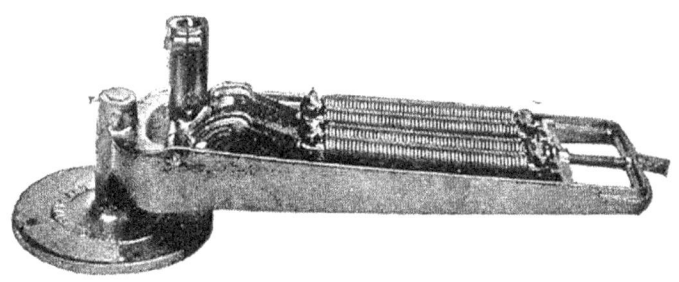

FIG. 20.

straight horizontal rod which slides along under the trolley wire.

The brake staff used on nearly all electric cars is very simple. However, the arrangement of levers on different makes of trucks varies greatly, and as a knowledge of the brake and how to use it is one of the most important things for a motorman to know, the subject of brakes will also be taken up in a chapter by itself.

To make our examination of a motor car equipment complete we have yet to notice two overhead or "canopy" switches, usually located under the hood above the platform on each end of the car. Pushing the handle of either one of these to the "off" position opens the circuit and cuts off all the current to controllers and motors, just as if the trolley wheel had been pulled from the wire, so that the motors and controllers may be safely examined and handled. A small switch is usually located inside the car near one door for turning the lamps on and off. If the car has electric heaters another switch is also provided for turning them on and off. A fuse box or an automatic circuit breaker will usually be found upon a car. The purpose of each of these devices is to automatically open the electric circuit whenever the amount of current used becomes so large that it will injure the motors. The construction and action of these devices will be explained in a subsequent chapter. Somewhere upon the car (usually beneath it) will be found a safety device called a lightning arrester which is intended to prevent lightning from reaching the motors. As lightning readily pierces any insulating material, this device is designed to deflect the lightning into the ground before it reaches or passes through the motors.

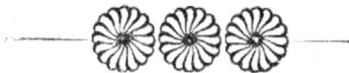

CHAPTER II.

TRANSMITTING ELECTRIC POWER.

In order to convey electric power to a distance certain precautions are necessary. The electric current has to be guided by means of a conductor, which in practice is generally copper wire, and in order that the energy transmitted shall be wasted as little as possible the conducting wire must be thoroughly insulated from the earth and from all other conducting bodies. It was found at an early day that there is a great deal of difference in conductivity between different substances, and that some conduct the current very easily, others less easily, and again others do not conduct the current at all unless it is forced through them under very high pressure. The first class of substances, which are known as good electrical conductors, includes all metals, and of the metals the best conductors are silver and copper. The last class of materials, which do not conduct electric current, are called non-conductors or insulators, and if a conductor is attached or supported upon a non-conducting substance the conductor is insulated from the ground to which the current tends to flow in the endeavor to establish an equilibrium of the forces acting. Thus, if we should lay bare electric wires in the ground we would receive but little current at the far end because the earth is itself a conductor of electricity and would absorb the greater part of the current in the wire. It is evident therefore that the conductor must be insulated from the earth and from all other conductors in order to transmit the current to a distant point where it is to be consumed. Perfectly dry air is one of the best insulators known, while water containing dissolved salts and other impurities, as generally found, is an excellent conductor. There is little chance for current to escape from a wire supported on insulating material unless moisture, acids or dirt is to be found on the surface of the insulators, in which case a slight leakage through the dirt or moisture will occur.

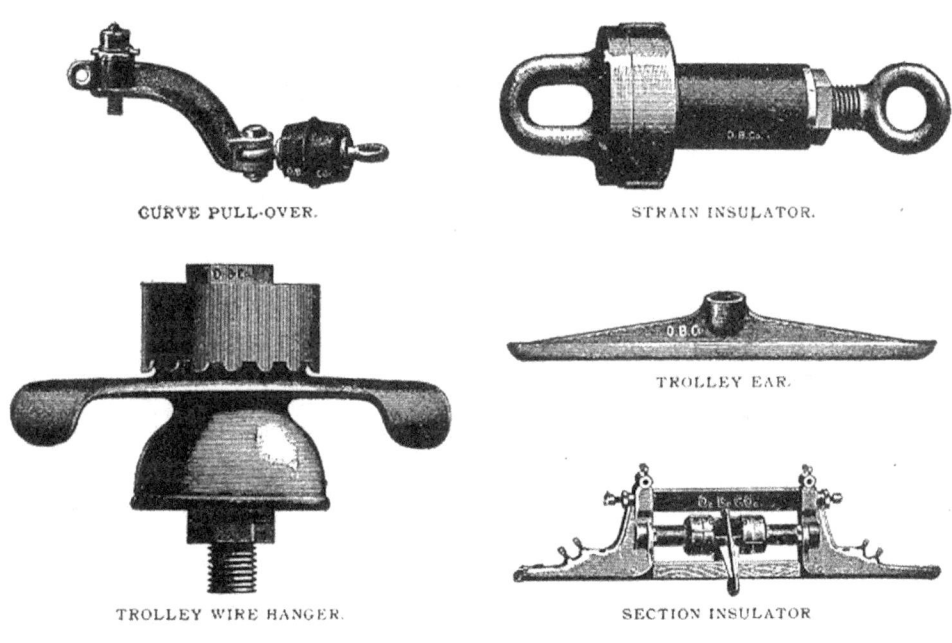

FIG. 21.

The best and most commonly used insulating substances are porcelain, glass, mica, rubber, dry wood, silk, shellac, paper, cotton, etc.

To transmit electricity from one place to another a certain amount of energy has to be spent in the transmission which is no longer available for useful work. This loss of energy is due to the resistance of the conductor which carries the current, and will be readily understood by the analogy of water flowing through a pipe. If we transmit a volume of water to a distance through a pipe under a certain pressure the pressure of the water at the further end of the pipe will be considerably less than the pressure at the point where the water enters the pipe. This loss of pressure is due to the friction of the water against the walls of the pipe and it will be readily seen is greater the greater the length of the pipe, and will be less for a given volume of water as the size of the pipe is larger. In the same way with an electric current, the longer the conducting wire the greater will be the resistance, while by increasing the diameter of the wire the resistance will be reduced. The smaller the amount of loss in the transmitting lines the more economical is the working of the system.

We have spoken of the volume, pressure and resistance of water in a pipe as being analagous to volume, pressure and resistance of current flowing through a conductor. The electrical unit of quantity corresponding to the volume of water is called the ampere. The electrical unit of pressure is called the volt, and the unit of electrical resistance is the ohm. According to Ohm's law the current in amperes equals the pressure in volts divided by the resistance in ohms. This laws is generally expressed by the equation:

$$C = \frac{E}{R}$$

in which C = current in amperes
E = electromotive force in volts
R = resistance in ohms

The electric current has to be produced in most cases by operating a dynamo by means of a steam engine, and this engine receives its energy from the boiler under which coal is burned. The energy located in the coal is utilized to evaporate the water in the boiler and the steam so produced actuates the engine, which in turn operates the dynamo. The greater the waste in electricity, the greater will be the coal consumption per month. Therefore, engineers strive to avoid losses as much as possible, such as leakage on electric lines or faults or leakage on devices connected therewith, as they form part of the circuit the moment the current is allowed to pass into them. For this reason motors, controllers and other parts attached to the car are highly insulated, and the overhead conductor is held in position by insulators, of hard rubber, glass, porcelain, compounds of mica, or other substances put into suitable shape under great pressure. Some such insulators as used on electric railways are

FIG. 22.

shown in Fig. 21. In most cases they consist of two metallic parts which are separated from one another by a strong and heavy layer of insulation. The one metallic part is then connected to the conductor which is to carry the electric current, while the other is attached to a pole, or span wire. This latter may be regarded as connected to the earth, but the other end is insulated from such contact by the interposed layer of non-conducting material. Fig. 22 shows such an insulator in section disclosing its construction.

The various steps in the generation and use of the electric current may be enumerated as in the following manner: Fig. 23 shows a boiler room of a street railway station and the steam here generated is conducted by the steam mains or pipes to the engine and dynamo room, Fig. 24. In

FIG. 23.

FIG. 24.

neary every station the arrangement of machines is different; in some, the engine drives the dynamo by means of a belt, but in most of the larger stations the dynamo is now direct connected, or in other words the armature of the dynamo is carried on the engine shaft, as shown in Fig. 25. The current is controlled by the use of a switchboard through which the dynamos are connected to the feeders or outgoing wires. Fig. 26 represents switchboard in a street railway station, upon which are switches for opening

FIG. 25.

and closing circuits, circuit breakers for protecting the dynamos from overloads, voltmeters for indicating the voltage and ammeters for indicating the amount of current flowing through the circuits.

The electrical transmission from a railway power station is shown in diagram in Fig. 27. To the left will be noticed the dynamo, which is connected by means of a commutator brush to the trolley wire (all switches, circuit breakers, safety devices, etc., at the station and on the car have been omitted for the sake of clearness and simplicity). Each electric car is indicated by one motor, wheel, trolley and controller. By following the arrows it will be observed that

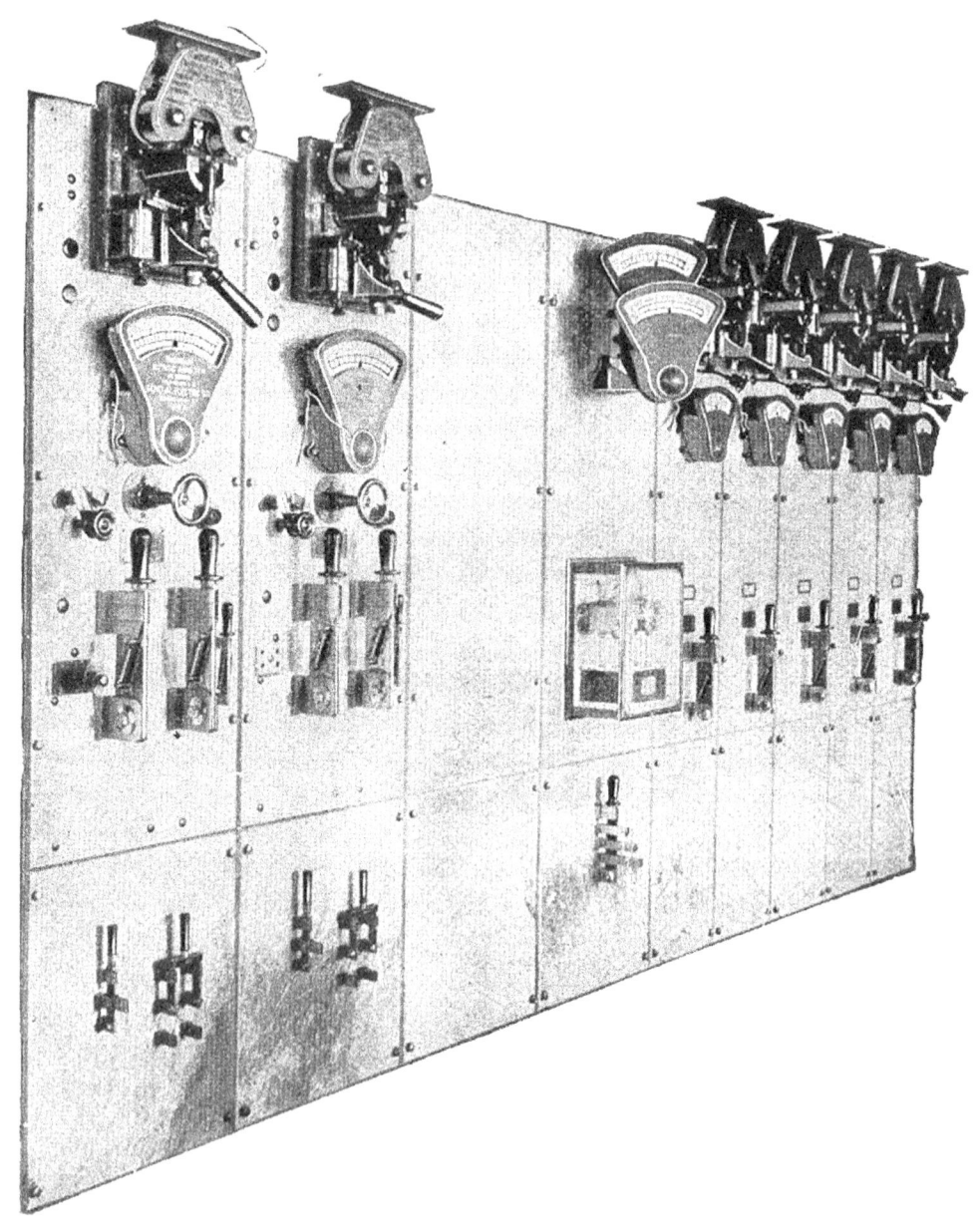

FIG. 26.

the electric current starts from the dynamo, goes to the trolley wire, from there to the trolley wheels and to the controllers; from the controllers to the motors, the windings of which are indicated by a few turns, and from there to the iron body of the motor, to the car wheel and to the rail. Through the rails and return feeders it flows back to

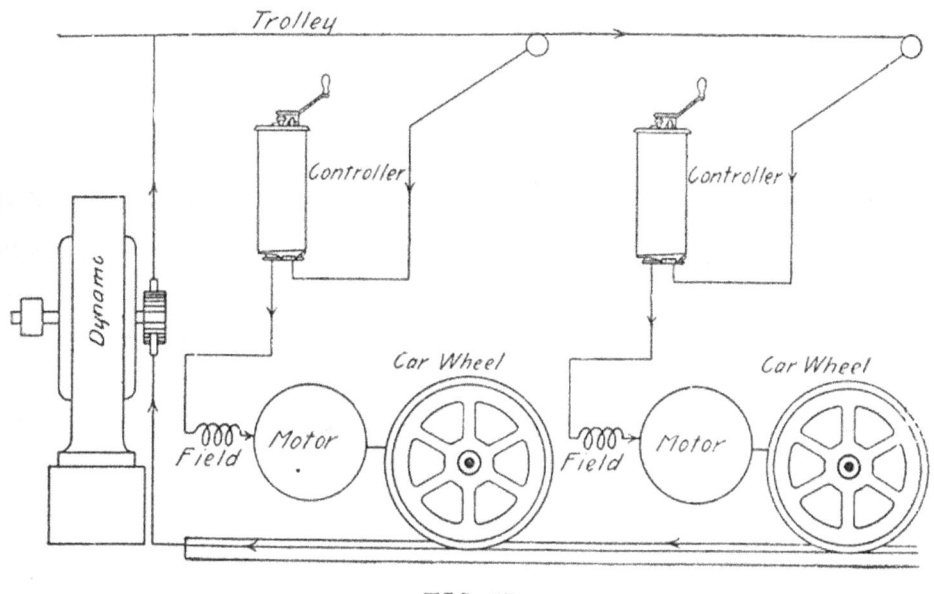

FIG. 27.

the station, where the second brush of the dynamo is connected to the rail. This completes a circuit, through the dynamo, out over the trolley wire, down through the motor and back through the rails, and current flows over this circuit whenever a controller is put in operation.

A SUGGESTION REGARDING POWER CONSUMPTION.

"A test made by the author between a good and a poor motorman, with the same motor car and same load, tested on the same dry summer day, showed that the better man used but one-half of the power taken by the other. What became of the other energy used by one of the men?" *The Motorman and His Duties: Page 40.*

The accompanying diagram answers the question.

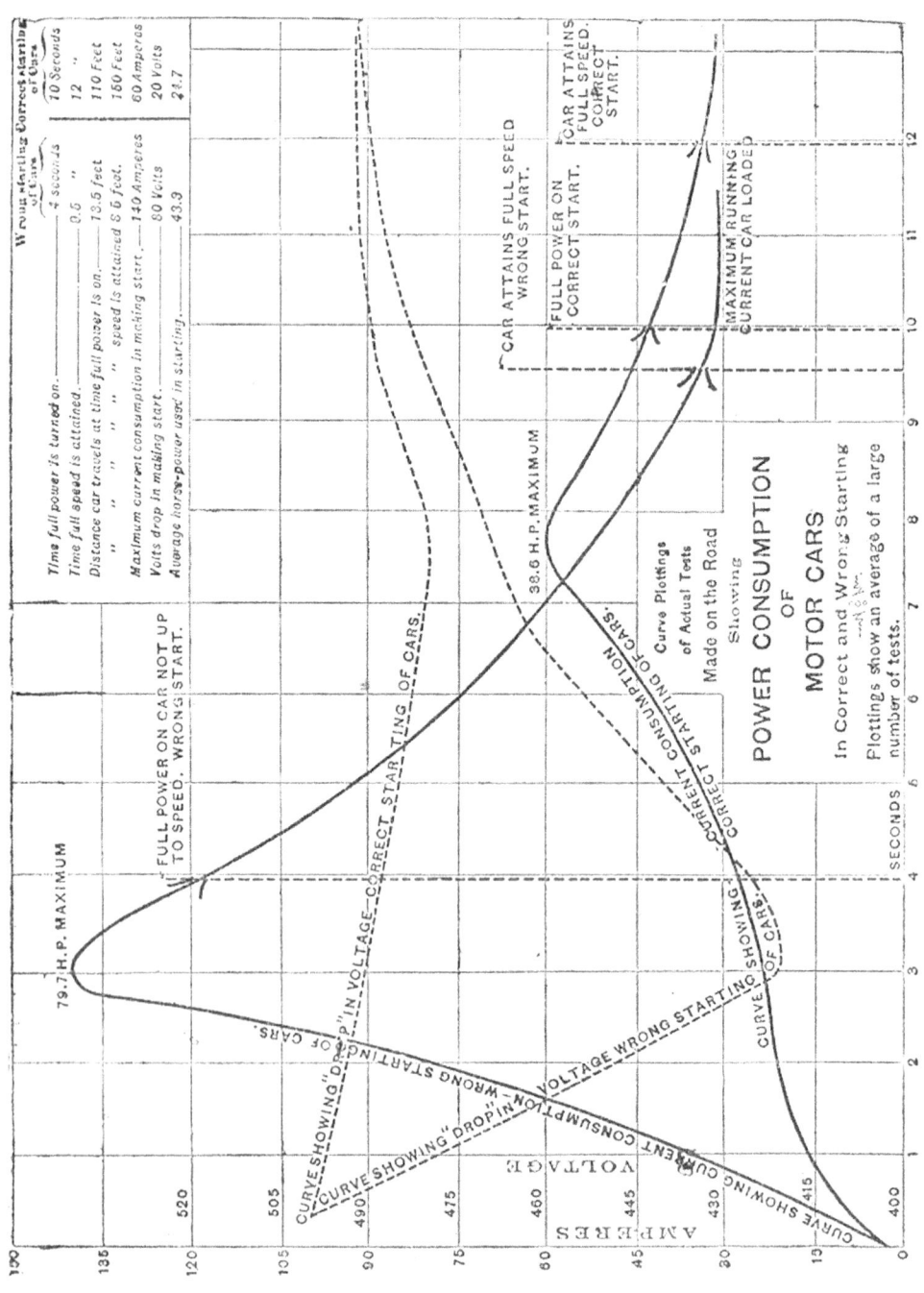

CHAPTER III.

OPERATION OF CARS AND CONTROLLERS.

The value of any motorman depends on the economy with which he can operate his car; economy in the way of preventing costly accidents, economy in power and economy in wear and tear of the cars, trucks and motors he runs. What has been said before has been intended to prepare the reader for this chapter, which deals directly with a motorman's actual duties. It does not require any special knowledge to be able to get a car over the road. To operate it in the best possible manner is quite another matter. It is the main object of this book to tell a motorman how to make himself a valuable man; how to operate a car with greatest economy.

Let us first learn something about the operation of controllers, beginning with the series-parallel controllers which are in common use today. The operation of all the controllers is very simple. They all have reverse levers at the right of the stand or on the top, and the controlling handle on all is moved around in the direction of the hands of a watch to turn on the current, and in the opposite direction to turn off the current. Before trying to start a car, first be sure that the brakes are off, that the controller handle at the other end of the car is on the "off" position and the canopy switches are closed. Then move the controller handle to the first notch. The car will start if all is right. After the car is well under way on the first notch, move to the second, and so on to the last. In moving from one notch to another do not stop the handle between notches, but give it a push strong enough so that it will go to the next notch. A timid or inexperienced motorman is apt to turn the handle slowly, but this is bad practice.

Always wait long enough on each notch for the car to gain speed before passing to the next notch. If you do not do this, much more current than necessary may be used to move the car. The wheels may slip, the motors will be strained and overheated and there will be a great drain on the power house generators, and wear on machinery. When the notch is reached where the motors are in series and there is no rheostat resistance in the circuit, special care should be taken to let them gain speed and run up to nearly the maximum speed they can attain in this position before passing to the higher notches where the motors are in parallel. When the motors are thrown in parallel too soon in starting, a waste of power takes place. This notch on which the motors are in series with no rheostat resistance in the circuit is the third point on the Westinghouse G, No. 14, No. 28, No. 29, the Walker J, and the General Electric K controllers. It is the fourth point on the General Electric K-2, the Westinghouse No. 28-A and No. 38, the Walker S and the Steel Motor Company's C controllers. It is on this series point that the motors exert the greatest pull with the least current, and it should preferably be used when there is heavy pulling to be done or steep grades to be climbed.

On looking at the points marked on the controller tops, we see that some of them are marked with longer or heavier marks than the others. Those points with long marks are called "running" points, because on them the motors may be operated for any length of time without overheating or wasting current in the rheostats. Among these running points there are some to be preferred because on them the whole energy taken into the motors is used to propel the car. These preferred points are those positions on which no rheostat resistance or diverter is left in circuit with the motors.

The K and K-2 controllers have four preferred running points. On the K controller the first preferred running point reached is the third, at which the motors are in series and resistance all cut out. This should be used for slow running. It gives a little less than half full speed. The fourth or next point is also a running position. It gives half full speed and may be used for running along on a level, but should never be used on a grade or for heavy pulling. The sixth point on the K controller is also a preferred running point, as is the seventh. The latter should only be used for highest speed on a level, as on it the fields are shunted, as on the fourth point. On the K-2 controller, the fourth and fifth and the eighth and ninth points are the preferred running points. The fourth here corresponds to the third on the K controller and the fifth here to the fourth on the K, and the fifth should be used in the same way as the fourth on the K. The eighth and ninth points of the K-2 are the high speed points, the ninth being only for use on a level. Use of the fifth or ninth points on grades is very wasteful of current and hard on the motors, and little is gained by it in the way of speed. The same is true of the fourth and seventh points on the K controller.

In the Westinghouse controllers, the third point in the G, No. 14, No. 28, No. 28-A and 29 is the first preferred position. In the No. 38 Westinghouse it is the fourth, in which the motors are in series without resistance. In the J controller of the Walker Company it is the third point, and in that of the Steel Motor Company it is the fourth point.

The second preferred running position in all of them is when the motors are at maximum speed. The Steel Motor

Company has on some motors and controllers a third such point, that is point 9, which is used when a shunt is provided in the field magnet winding of the motors.

In shutting off current the controller handle should be brought rapidly to the off position from whatever point it may happen to be on, without stopping at any point. To run the car backward when it is standing, pull the reverse lever back and turn on the current as when running forward. Sometimes it is necessary to reverse when the car is running ahead, to avoid running into something. To do this, throw controller handle to "off" and pull back reverse handle. Then move controller to the first notch. The car will stop with a jerk and begin to go backward. This way should be resorted to only when there is danger, and even then the car speed should be slow, because it is not a sure remedy. The fuse may blow and so suddenly shut off the power on account of the abnormally heavy current flowing. There is also a possibility that one or the other motor may be permanently disabled.

There is, however, one way in which a violent stop can be made with a series-parallel controller, even when the power is cut off and the brakes fail. It is done by reversing and putting the controller handle on the highest point of the controller. In this case the motors act as dynamos, generating current. This method may be used in emergencies when the brakes are not sufficient and the trolley has come off or the fuse has blown and the car is going down an incline. You may never have to use it, and it is not creditable to have to use it by letting a car get beyond control. But the brake may give out or something else happen beyond the control of the motorman, so it should always be remembered, as it may save you a sad accident some day. In case you have reversed and the fuse blows, the instant you feel that the power has been shut off by the blowing of the fuse, put your controller around on one of the higher points named. This plan may also be used in case the brakes fail and the trolley comes off going down hill. It is a very violent way of stopping, and injurious to the equipment. On the Walker S controller the emergency brake notch on the reverse switch should be used instead of reversing, as explained in chapter on controllers in Part II.

The Westinghouse D controller, the old Edison and Sprague controllers are different both in construction and operation from the series-parallel controllers just mentioned. When their handles are at "off" they point straight backwards. There is no separate reverse lever. Turning the handle to the left from the off position runs the car forward. Turning the handle to the right runs the car backward. In starting a car with the Westinghouse D controllers, advance the handle firmly from notch to notch, as with the series-parallel controller, pausing after each notch long enough to let the car get up to speed.

On the top of the Edison and Sprague controllers points are cast which indicate the contact positions on the controller drum. The motorman should stop long enough in each position to allow the motor to get up to speed. Reversing or running backwards is accomplished in all of these controllers simply by moving the handle around from "off" to the right side of the controller. Of course the same precautions should be observed about reversing as with the other controllers, that is, reverse only in great emergency, and then only to the first point, after having first brought the handle to the off position and reducing the speed by applying the hand brake.

When there are two motors on a car, an emergency stop can be made when the trolley is off or the fuse is blown by reversing to the highest point. In shutting off current on these controllers be careful not to go past the "off" position onto the reverse side of the controller.

The early controllers of the General Electric Company have all been of the T. H. rheostat type, as shown in Fig. 72. It consists of a double lever on each platform and a crescent or half circular resistance box below the platform, over which a contact shoe having a number of fingers is made to slide by the operating or controlling handle. The second lever has two positions, a forward and a backward position. It is the reversing switch and should be pushed to the extreme end of its position. This switch lever is easily distinguished from the rheostat lever by standing out horizontally.

To start the car the handle should be turned from left to right, or (looking down on it) turned in the same direction as the hands of a watch. There is a stop at both extremities, beyond which it cannot be turned. When the car is to be stopped the handle must be turned backwards, or from right to left once, twice or more (depending on the position of the handle), until it cannot be turned any farther. It is not sufficient that the contact shoe be removed from the resistance box, but the handle should be moved until it reaches the stop.

In starting, turn on the current slowly, moving the handle a little ways at a time. Shutting off the current should be done by rapidly turning the handle back to the "off" position. Reversing is accomplished the same way as with the series-parallel controllers. Never reverse unless the current is first shut off.

HINTS ON SAVING POWER.

It is not necessary that a man be powerful to control an electric car. At first he is apt to spend an unnecessary amount of energy at the brake. Power may be saved and the car would be subject to less wear and tear if handled not by pure strength, but by proper judgment of time and distance. It should be considered that as long as the controller is not on the "off" position power is taken into the motors and consumed. If a car is to be stopped, turn off the power some time ahead, because the energy taken into the motor does not disappear the moment you shut off the current. The motors and the car have weight, and energy is stored in this moving body and this energy must be spent before the car can come to rest. Some men, because they have not the right judgment, set the brake the moment the controller is placed at the "off" position, and they must then work hard at the brake and consume the energy still stored in the moving car, by spending it partly in wear on themselves, brake shoes, car wheels, motors and gears. It means a wear all around, without a benefit to anyone.

A test made by the author between a good and a poor motorman with the same motor car and same load, tested on the same dry summer day, showed that the better man used but one-half the power taken by the other. What became of the other energy used by one of the men? You would soon know if you were frequently around the barn. The man who uses the most power seems tired when he goes home in the evening, from the hard work he had at the brake. You would know it by observing the greater wear on brake shoes and constant trouble with brakes, softer car wheels, which soon wear flat in spots, and frequent loose bolts on cars operated by men of no experience or poor judgment. The simplest thing in the world is to cut off your power ahead of time and let the energy stored in the car spend itself by allowing it to propel the car by its momentum for half a block or so, and you will be surprised how easily it can be stopped by setting the brake. What has been said here, however, is not always possible to do, and a motorman must use his judgment. For instance, if the pressure or voltage is low, or many stops have to be made, or the motors have not speed enough for the schedule time set by the company, a motorman cannot act exactly as he would wish, but in these cases the conditions are not normal. Such rules can be used as a guide when a road is properly equipped and the schedule time for a round trip is so chosen compared with the distance to be covered and speed of the motors that the motors can accomplish their work easily.

When running up behind a team on the track and you see that you will overtake it before it gets out of the way, do not crowd your car up to speed and rush up behind it, as is often done, only to be obliged to put the brakes on hard to avoid a collision. You will make just as good time and save your muscle and the company's power by letting your car run along slowly enough to get the team out of the way before you reach it instead of bringing your car almost to a stop after having run up to it at full speed.

Should the wheels slip or skid on going up grade, bring your sand box into action, and if the car wheels continue to slip then throw the controller handle to the "off" position and turn it on again step by step. When the rail is greasy or covered with snow so that the wheels do not take hold of the rail, apply a little sand before starting the car. Use the sand sparingly and be sure that you have some left when in need of it.

SOME PRECAUTIONS AGAINST ACCIDENTS.

When approaching curves, switches, turn outs or railroad crossings slow down your car so as to have it under control. It is best to have the controller at the "off" position and the right hand on the brake. The moment the wheels reach the curve, switch or crossing you may put on your power gradually, to carry the car over the curve or crossing. Never let the car stop in a short curve, such as is frequently found on country roads, unless there are special instructions by the authority of your road. When taking curves or turn outs the conductor should be on the rear platform ready to replace the trolley should it jump the wire. If the trolley passes the curve or switch properly, the conductor should ring "go ahead"; if the trolley jumps he should ring "stop." If the conductor has given his signal that the trolley has jumped off the wire, the motorman should keep his controller handle at the "off" position until the conductor rings "go ahead."

When going around curves, crossings or other places where the car may jump the track owing to roughness of road-bed, or where rails are laid very low in a gravel road, and where stones may wedge in the rails, slow speed should be used, as also when passing through flooded places or low places where the rails are covered with water. When going up grades, it is best to put the controller on points where the resistance is cut out, and further, the car should not be stopped or started on a grade if it can be avoided.

When passing an overhead insulated switch or section insulator, place your controller always at the "off" position, unless you are on a grade or have other instructions from the superintendent.

Going down grade have your controller handle at the "off" position, the trolley on the trolley wire and your brake set to such an extent that the wheels turn slowly (not slide) so that the car remains under your control, slackening the hold on the wheels when the grade becomes less steep or tightening the grip of the brake shoes should the grade become steeper. Should the car get beyond your control or the brake suddenly give out, you may have to resort to reversing the controller, as previously explained.

It is a severe strain on the motors, but may have to be resorted to, to prevent an accident or to save lives. When so reversing keep the controller in the first notch should it be effective; if not, turn the handle very slowly to the higher notches, as the fuse is liable to give out and your control by means of current from the power house is gone. Should the fuse blow there is then, as before mentioned, only one more means to get the car under control, and that is to throw the controller to the last notch, which causes the motors to act as dynamos. This plan is only available when there are two motors on a car. The current is generated by the rotation of the armature in the field. The energy furnished is the momentum of the descending car, which is out of your control and disconnected from the power house. The current so generated acts by means of the armatures as a brake and the car will slow up in the same measure, as the motors generate current. The means just described are important to know, but should never be resorted to except in extreme cases.

When stopping a car in the barn pull down the trolley one foot or a foot and a half and tie it, also see that both controllers are on the "off" position and open the overhead or canopy switch. If for any reason the trolley should be left on the wire in the barn some of the car lamps might be turned on, which will be a warning to the repair men.

Before starting see that the controllers on both platforms are on the "off" position. Never place tools, rubber boots or other wearing apparel, cotton waste or the like on the side below the seat where the motor cut out or wire cable connecting controllers and motors are located. Keep this place clean and free from dirt and moisture.

When examining motors open your main or overhead switch and take care not to let water drop into the motor from wet clothing. When examining car motors, fuse, etc., always open the overhead switch to avoid shocks. When operating a car, any unusual noise heard should be located. Loose bolts should be reported and attended to, because by the fixing in proper time of these small irregularities, which are caused by jarring and constant operation of the car, grave trouble can be prevented, and a car will remain much longer in good repair if kept so and watched.

It is true that a stitch in time saves nine. The writer has seen plants, where cars were neglected, bolts could be picked up along the road, and on one occasion a car was stalled because the lower half of a field magnet had dropped down and was wedged against the stone pavement. Should a motorman notice irregularities or defects on the overhead line or on the track the matter should be reported.

When operating on a road with steep grades be sure that you are prepared in damp or slippery weather to be able to get sand from the boxes. It is not sufficient to see that there is sand in them, but that you know it is dry sand and that the valve is in such condition that it will let the sand pass through.

Never shift the reversing handle unless the controller handle is on the "off" position, nor reverse when the car is in motion except to prevent an accident.

When leaving the platform be sure your controller is turned off and remove your controller handle. Keep them in your hand should you be on the road, and in the barn you should leave them, according to the rules given by the company. The reason the motorman should not leave the controller handle on the controller is that accidents are encouraged. The author has frequently seen that at country fairs, where people crowd into the cars at both ends, people are apt to strike the handle with baskets or coats held over the arm, and can in this way start the car unexpectedly. Keeping the handle in one's hand on such occasions leaves the motorman in full control of his car and up to the requirements of his duty and responsibility.

Young people do not realize the responsibility of the position of a motorman; they may think it fun to hide the handle when he has left the car for a moment. Such liberties have been taken by people who knew the motorman when a car, for instance, was at the end of a track and had to wait for 5 or 10 minutes. As the motorman is held responsible for his car he should therefore always have it under full control, and leave it so no one can accidentally start it.

Should at any time you feel that the power gives out in the power house, for instance, by the operating of a circuit breaker, then bring your controller handle to the "off" position, close your lamp circuit and wait until the lamps light.

Before starting the car for your run, see that your brushes and brush springs are in position (unless there is some one else whose duty it is to keep the cars in readiness for the motorman). Before placing the trolley on the wire, look at both controllers and be sure that they are both at the "off" position. Do not run the car with the trolley pole in the wrong direction, because in this position it has no yielding properties when it strikes a hanger or suspension wire. If it jumps the wire it would bend the pole or cause trouble to the overhead wire.

When starting as a motorman in a new town or on a new road it is well to ride once or twice over the road as a passenger or with another motorman in charge of the car to give you a chance to get a general idea of the road, the location of switches, turn outs, railway crossings, bridges, etc.

The operation of the brakes is one of the most important duties of a motorman and one of the most difficult. Accordingly, it is treated in a chapter by itself.

CHAPTER IV.

OPERATION OF BRAKES.

A number of brake mechanisms are described in the chapter on brakes, Part II, for the purpose of learning the operation. The description of the adjustment is given more particularly for those motormen operating cars on the small country roads where frequently they are called upon to attend to such mechanical matters. In large cities and on large roads special inspectors are provided, and the author wishes to impress especially on those motormen who have inventive faculties, or imagine they have, or those who like to do tinkering, that they should touch absolutely nothing about the car equipment unless ordered by the road officers or regulations to do so. The company cannot afford to have a man experiment with its cars, especially when mechanics are employed to attend to all irregularities on car or truck. Inasmuch as this book is intended to tell a man how he should qualify himself for the position, it must not only tell him how to get a position but also how to keep it. You will certainly lose your position if the company finds out that you tamper with any mechanical or electrical part. Playing or tinkering must be entirely avoided if you want to be able to stay for any length of time with any company. However much a man might desire to fix his car, it is not worth while to risk his position if he acts against the rules of the company in doing so.

While starting your car from the barn try the brakes, to see if they are right. Always be sure your brakes are fully off before starting your controller. On grades it will be necessary to start the controller the instant the brake is released. There is usually some slack in the brake chain with hand brakes unless the shop men keep them closely adjusted.

It should be the constant effort of the motorman to avoid locking the wheels so that they slide or skid along the rail. There are two good reasons for this. In the first place, the instant the wheels begin to slide on the rails the braking or retarding force is reduced, or what is the same, the motorman loses more than half his retarding power. This has been fully proved by experiment and by experience. In the second place, there is danger that by this sliding along the rails a flat place will be worn on the wheels. Such flat places will pound with every turn of the wheels and rapidly grow worse, so that the noise becomes unbearable to the public and the wheels must be turned down at considerable expense or thrown away. A flat wheel on a car is, therefore, no credit to a motorman, and on some roads the penalty for a flat wheel is suspension. It is often hard to avoid sliding the wheels when sleet or mud is on the rails, but this should be remembered above all, viz., never turn on sand after the wheels have commenced to slide without first letting up on the brakes so that the wheels can turn. The safer plan when stopping on a slippery rail is to apply sand at the same time you apply the brakes. Remember that you cannot stop as quick by sliding the wheels as you can by putting on brakes firmly without sliding them. In coming to a steep down grade be sure to slow up your car before reaching the incline and set your brakes gradually. If the wheels get to sliding on the grade loosen up on the brakes until they begin to turn again. Cars have run away down hills because motormen have lost their heads or failed to know and remember this point.

The wear or lasting qualities of the brake shoes and the power taken from the power plant by a motorman to run a car depends to a considerable extent on his proper judgment of time and distance. The less he absorbs the stored energy with the brake, the smaller will be the wear on brake shoes and car wheels and the smaller the power taken.

It is not a good plan to make gradual stops by applying the brakes lightly a long distance back of where you want to stop, as you lose time in getting over the road in this way and require more power in making up for it. Let the car drift with brake entirely off until a short distance from the stopping place, and then apply them hard enough to make a comparatively short stop without sliding the wheels or making it uncomfortable for the passengers.

CHAPTER V.

HOW TO REMEDY TROUBLES.

On many large roads the motormen are expected to do nothing beyond operating their cars, and whenever trouble occurs to a car on the road it is pushed in by the next and the repair men at the barn attend to the repairing. A motorman should of course always abide by the rules of his company, and if they forbid the opening of motors or controllers by motormen the author does not mean these instructions to in any way interfere with rules which may seem necessary to the officers of large systems where the motormen are not all well posted and where inspectors are employed whose special work it is to remedy slight troubles and where mischief may be done by the tampering of those who do not understand the apparatus. Nevertheless, there are many small roads where a knowledge of how to remedy troubles is needed, and even on the large roads mentioned the man who understands his car can save many delays and knows how to report troubles intelligently.

In enumerating many of the troubles to which the cars and motors are subject and giving instructions for their temporary remedy, the author wishes to place in the hands of the motorman facts and means which are helpful for such an occasion. However, no one should think that without practical experience, by simply reading these lines, that he can manage a car as well as a man who has been operating one for years. Practical experience is absolutely necessary, but in connection with it this chapter will be very helpful to the motorman.

A great deal must be learned by actual experience, and success in economical operation on a car line depends partly on the watchfulness of the motorman. While operating his controller he can readily detect irregularities, first, by the way the motors take the current when the controller is operated, and secondly, when the car is under way, by the sound of the motors.

The economy which can thus be accomplished lies in the fact that loose bolts, a loose connection and the like are easily tightened. These are small troubles caused by constant jarring of the car, which are easily attended to. However, if the car is not watched bolts will be lost, bearings will come loose, the armature revolving at a great rate of speed may be rubbing against the field magnet poles, or a wire working out of its connection may cause a short circuit and blow the fuse, etc. It will be readily seen that these small troubles, if not attended to in time, are the causes of others far more serious, yet a turn of the wrench or the screwdriver in proper time may easily prevent such troubles on the road. The golden rule, "a stitch in time saves nine," should be remembered at all times, and besides this one, "cleanliness is next to Godliness." Keep your motors, connections and contact terminals clean and dry. Before working around the electrical apparatus pull off trolley and open overhead switch.

If the car fails to start when the controller is "on" and both overhead switches are closed, the trouble is due to an open circuit, and probably to one of the following causes:

1. The fuse may have blown or melted. Open an overhead switch or pull off the trolley and put in a new fuse, removing the burned ends from under the binding posts before doing so. Never put in a heavier fuse than that

specified by the company, as it might result in damage to the equipment by allowing too large a current to flow. The fuse may blow because of some trouble on the car, as will be explained a little further on.

2. On a dry summer day, when there is much fine dust on the track, it happens that the car wheels do not make proper contact with the rail and the car fails to start. In such a case try to establish contact by rocking the car body. Should this fail to work, the conductor should take the switch bar or a piece of wire and, holding one end firmly on a clean place on the rail, hold the other against the wheel or truck. This will make temporary connection until the car has started. The conductor should be sure to make his rail contact first and keep it firm during this operation or he may receive a shock.

3. If the track conditions are apparently good, it may be that the car stands on a piece of dead rail—a piece of rail on which the bonding has become destroyed. In that case the car conductor would have to go to the next rail section with a piece of wire to connect the two rails and then order the motorman to start his car.

4. Another outside trouble which the author has noticed, especially on cars having wooden trolley poles, is that, due to the constantly varying pressure on the pole, the wire connecting the trolley wheel with the trolley base breaks off short near the place where the trolley head or fork is mounted. In such a case wrap a bare piece of wire around the lower part of the trolley fork and continue it around the wooden pole, and be sure to establish good connection between the wire you place temporarily round the pole and that one running down to the trolley base. This latter irregularity can be noticed by the motorman, because the current taken into the car is irregular. Sometimes the motors get the power properly; at other times

they start slowly as if they did not receive the proper current. In the evening it can be noticed by the slight arcing that takes place between the broken ends.

5. A brush or two may not have been placed, or if placed, may fit too tightly in the brush holder, so that the springs do not establish contact between brush and commutator. If this is the case, remove brushes and sandpaper them until they go into the brush holder easily.

6. The contact fingers on a controller are rough, burnt, and perhaps bent so that the drum cannot make contact. Try to remove burnt surface with sandpaper and bend fingers or contacts into their proper position. Should this fail, then operate the car with the other controller. In this case the conductor should be on the front platform to handle the brake and give orders to the motorman when to start and stop, as the occasion requires. Under these conditions the car should never be allowed to travel at a high speed. It may also be due to wear on both the contact surfaces of the drum and the finger, which may have been burnt and worn away to such an extent that contact is not established when the controller handle is placed on the first notch.

7. A loose or broken cable connection. This can be located and placed and fastened in its position. It is, in most instances, a cable connected to one of the motors, rheostat, or lightning arrester and very seldom in the controller stand.

8. A burnt rheostat. A rheostat may have received too great a current for some time and the first contact terminal may be broken. In such a case, if temporary connection cannot conveniently be established, the car will not start at the first notch, but at the second it will start with a jerk.

9. If car refuses to start on the first contact, but starts

all right on the second and acts normal thereafter, then there is an open circuit in the rheostat, either internally, or the first cable connection is broken. It may also be due to a worn controller and the contacts may be blistered or burnt. Move the controller handle slightly beyond the notch or go direct to the second notch.

10. The field coil of a motor may be grounded so that the fuse blows whenever current is turned on. Cut out the faulty motor, as explained in Chapter III, Part II.

11. Armature or commutator grounded. Cut out motor as in 10.

12. Lightning arrester is grounded by dirt between the discharge points. Remove the dirt, as the fuse will blow as long as the trouble exists. Should this not be possible then disconnect the lightning arrester, ground wire, insert fuse and go ahead. The trouble lies in the arrester.

13. The car starts and the fuse may blow. This may be due to a heavy load and the fuse not securely fastened to its terminals. The screws holding the terminals of the fuse should be tight, because loose contact at these points will cause heating and an increased resistance, and in consequence a quicker burning of the fuse.

14. Case 13 may happen with comparatively few passengers. The load may be caused artificially by having the brakes partially set or dirt clogging between the brake shoes and car wheels. Remove obstruction between brake shoes, then insert fuse.

15. In car equipments, with motors permanently in parallel, fuse will blow if a field or armature is short circuited. Proceed as in 10.

There are also other irregularities which may occur, as follows:

16. Some cables form a short circuit either under the seat or below controller due to dampness, dirt, damaged

insulation, etc. This can readily be detected by the smell of burnt rubber. Having found the place, first open your overhead switch, then proceed to wrap rubber tape around the bare place. If this is not on hand, use some dry cotton or woolen rag torn into a narrow band or else dry string. If the wires cannot be separated far enough, place some short pieces of dry wood between them and then tie them together.

17. The car starts and after the controller reaches a certain point fuse blows. One armature or a field is short circuited. Cut out the faulty motor and go on with the other.

18. The car starts, stops and starts again. This may be caused by a loose contact finger at the controller or by a loose cable or wire. Remove casing from controller, and if you see blisters on the drum of your controller examine the finger belonging to this particular contact, clean it and screw it home or bring it back to its normal form should it have been bent. If the controller looks all right the trouble may be found to be due to a loose cable connected to the terminals of a motor. Take screwdriver and tighten all cables going to the field coils, armature and brush holders. Also examine brushes. If your commutator looks dark and burnt it may be due to a brush, which has worn down to such an extent that the brush springs do not press it against the commutator. In this latter case substitute a new brush, but if none is at hand, cut out the motor and go ahead with the other.

19. The car starts with a jerk, but afterward runs smooth and normal. There is a short circuit probably in the rheostat. Examine the rheostat terminals and remove the trouble, which may be due to the crossing of the cables or a loose cable touching another terminal. Should the trouble be internal, namely, inside of the rheostat, you

should not touch it at all, but run your car back to the barns and report the defects.

20. A motor field or armature coil may be burned out. Cut out this motor, which can be detected by the smell of shellac and burnt cotton.

21. Should the speed of the motor increase beyond normal, a field magnet coil is either short circuited or burnt out. The motor should be cut out.

22. Should there be heavy flashing in the controller and smoking, it is due to dirt, moisture, metal dust in the controller, or too slow turning off of the controller. Open your overhead switch and blow out the dust from the ring terminals, remove also all dust at the lower ends of the controller and see that it is dry.

23. Should the lamps not light up on turning the lamp switch, see if your lamp circuit fuse is not burnt. If in good order either a lamp is not screwed home into its sockets or one of the lamps is burnt out. If one is burnt out none will light up, because they are in series.

There are also other irregularities which may occur which it is well for the motorman to understand, although he may not be able to remedy them.

24. One motor of a car becomes a great deal hotter than the other. This may be due to uneven distribution of work caused by difference in the magnetic circuit of the two motors, or to one set of wheels being smaller in diameter than the other, or a ground in the field coil or short circuit in the field coil of the hot motor.

25. Abnormal heating of one of the motor armatures may be due to its striking the field poles when rotating.

26. Heating of the motor may also be due to defective brake, caused by weak release springs or too short a brake chain.

27. Heating may be also due to the oil or grease used which does not melt properly, if at all. A full grease or oil cup is no sign of proper lubrication. If it is found that bearings heat, in spite of full grease cups, take a clean stick, make a hole through the grease down to the shaft, pour in soft oil and go ahead. It may not be a bad idea to occasionally feel the car axle bearings, which get pretty warm when insufficiently supplied with oil.

28. A sharp, rattling noise when the car is traveling at high speed is the consequence of an uneven commutator. A commutator that is flat in places, or a few bars that have become loose and project slightly, cause the brushes to be quickly forced away from the commutator by the high bars, and to be forced back onto the lower ones by the brush holder spring as soon as a high bar has passed. The rapid succession of these changes causes the noise, which should be reported. It causes heavy sparking at the brushes and excessive heating of the commutator segments, besides rapid wearing down of the brushes. This can be remedied only in the repair shop.

29. A dull thumping noise, also connected with sparking at the brushes, may be due to the armature striking or rubbing against the pole pieces. If this is due to loose bearings the cap bolts should be tightened, but if on account of wornout boxes, the car should be taken to the barn at a slow rate of speed, and reported without delay.

30. If the car starts with a jerk and the gears make considerable noise, the teeth of the pinion may be worn or fit loosely in the gear, or the key seat on the armature shaft has been made wider by the constant wear of a loose key. This trouble should be reported as soon as possible.

31. Loud noise from the gearing is sometimes due to loose gears, the teeth of which have too much play. It is increased if the gear casing is partially opened, caused by

loose bolts, or when they are removed entirely. The same trouble of improper meshing of teeth in the gears may be due to a bent armature shaft or a bent car axle. The trouble should be reported to the car inspector or other proper authority.

32. Another noise frequently heard is the thumping of a car wheel which has a flat spot. The trouble may be due to natural wear, or due to poor track, but most frequently due to improper handling of the brake, which is set too suddenly and prevents the wheels from turning. If the brake is set too tight when going down grade, it will cause the wheels to slide along the rails on four points, which, due to friction, become heated, with the result of softening that part of the wheel, which will wear rapidly into a flat place, causing a disagreeable hammering noise at every revolution of the wheel.

33. If the motors start with a jerk or do not run smoothly, the conductor should lift one of the trap doors at a time, while the car is running, to examine the commutator and brushes of each motor. Should there be seen a flash all around the commutator or connecting two brushes, then there is an open circuit in the armature. Cut out the motor and proceed on your trip with the other motor alone.

A short circuit on a motor in a car means that by some cause or defect a shorter circuit is found by the electric current other than is properly provided in the system, and it has the effect of weakening or disabling the part thus affected. For instance, assume that to make the magnet of a motor strong, there is placed around it 500 turns of wire; due to dampness or dirt, let there be cut out 300 or 400 turns; then a current will flow through but 100 turns; the circuit has become shorter than was intended by the designer. Such defects not only lead to irregularity in handling, but cause a strain on the dynamo in the power house. Every second that a motor runs after something is wrong is liable to greatly increase the damage. Therefore, cut out a defective motor the moment it is discovered. Short circuits can be caused by dirt and rain, by crossing of the flexible wires joined to the motors and in many other ways. A short circuit on a line means that nearly all or all the necessary resistance which a motor or other translating device should offer when in good condition has been removed by a defect, and now acts as a conductor of very little resistance connecting the two wires constituting the line. In a railway system this would mean a direct connection between trolley wire and rail, the current not properly passing through the motors.

A ground on a motor, or a short circuit, means that some part of the insulation has become defective and that the current has found its way to the iron core. In most railway systems used at present the trolley wire is one of the conductors, while the rails form the second or return conductor. A ground on a motor equipment indicates that a part of the field or the armature winding, through which the current should flow before reaching the car wheel, has been cut out of action by a defect. The car will then not operate as well, and depending on the seriousness of the defect, will go slower or faster than when in good order. If a ground cuts out a great deal of the motor circuit it is about equivalent to a short circuit. If a guard wire, telegraph or telephone wire should fall over the trolley wire and touch the ground it would establish an earth connection, which is equivalent to a short circuit on the dynamo.

Should a wire be found hanging over the trolley wire, but not reaching the ground, it should be removed with the greatest of care. It does not form a ground, as it may be several feet away from the ground; however, it is charged by touching the trolley wire. In trying to remove it with the bare hands, standing on the ground, the man who intends to give his services to remove the obstruction forms himself the rest of the circuit and establishes a ground through his body. The moment he would touch this apparently lifeless wire with his bare hands, the current discharges through his body into the ground.

A wire covered with rubber insulation can be handled, but even in this case the same precaution should be taken, as no one can tell how good the insulation may be. Frequently rubber insulation becomes brittle and hard when exposed to atmospheric changes—hot and cold weather, rain and snow—and in this state the insulation is worse than none, because persons may think the covering still to be an insulator when, in fact, it may be carbonized and itself a partial conductor. In damp weather and with high voltages, as now commonly used, such insulation should not be relied on and should be treated as if the wire was a bare one.

If you see the construction man on his tower wagon handle the trolley wire with bare hands, you should remember that he stands on a high wooden ladder, and he therefore is well insulated from the ground. Even in his lofty position he has to be on his guard, because the trolley suspension wires are in some cities connected to the iron poles without an insulator between them, only one insulator being provided, which is interposed between the trolley wire and the span. If he touches either one alone he is safe, but if he touches the trolley wire and at the same time this span wire attached to the iron pole, he establishes a connection from the trolley to the ground through his hands, arms and body and has to suffer the consequences. In most towns the trolley suspension wires are now insulated at both ends, so that they can be handled without danger.

It may happen that you have to handle a live trolley wire which has broken or fallen in the street, or a telephone or other wire which has fallen across the trolley wire. Never take hold of the wire with your bare hands. If you must take hold of it, put several thicknesses of clothing between your hands and it, if the cloth is dry. Otherwise, use sticks and a rope to remove it.

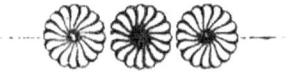

Part II.

CHAPTER I.

THE PRINCIPLES OF THE ELECTRIC MOTOR.

Many persons have the idea that a dynamo or an electric motor is so complicated a device that it takes years of study to understand it. Nothing is farther from the truth. The fact is, that it is built on one of the simplest principles, and if this principle is well understood it will be easy to understand any machine, because in analyzing we always go back to the simple principle and leave out the many complicated additions which may be attached to a machine for one reason or another.

A dynamo or motor is nothing else but a powerful mag-

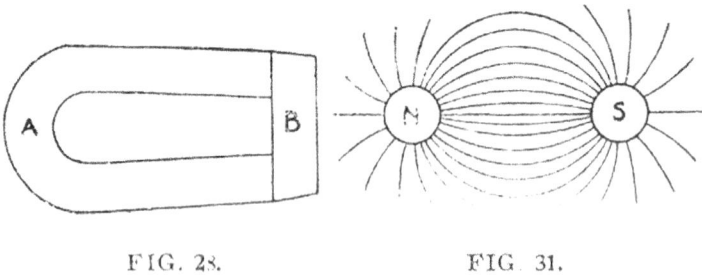

FIG. 28. FIG. 31.

net, and differs in principle but slightly from the common horseshoe magnet. Fig. 28 represents a magnet which we can buy in any hardware store. To understand the action of a dynamo or motor, it becomes necessary to understand this little magnet. It is a piece of flat steel bent into the form of a horseshoe, which is hardened and afterward magnetized. It has been found that steel, when hardened, will retain magnetism for a long time, that is, for months and years; provided, however, that it has constantly some work to do. For this reason the keeper B is always found with the magnet. The keeper or armature B is a simple piece of soft iron which, when brought near to the end of the magnet poles or the horseshoe, will be attracted and held

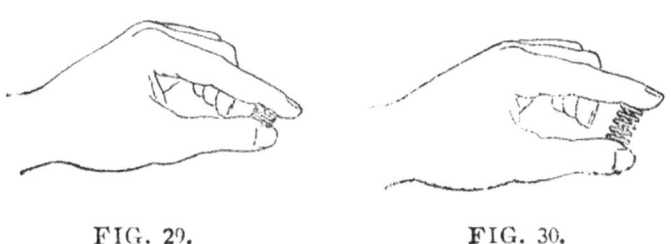

FIG. 29.   FIG. 30.

by the magnet. If we attempt to remove this piece of iron B from magnet A we find that it requires some force; that it takes energy to pull off the iron piece from the magnet. We are therefore confronted by the fact that this bent piece of steel has energy stored in it, and that this energy is capable of doing work. The magnet, which at first had to be charged, takes up energy which is stored in it, and which afterward it can return to do useful work. It is similar to a spiral spring. We have to spend energy to compress it (Fig. 29), but the moment we reduce the pressure we feel that the spring tries to utilize the stored energy and force our fingers apart (Fig. 30).

If we remove the armature from the horseshoe magnet, the energy acts from one end of the magnet to the other through the air. The energy or flow of energy is not visible to the eye, but the results of this force are made visible by the action of iron filings when brought near to a magnet. With the aid of iron filings it is found that this force is very intense near and between the ends of poles, and spread in curves the farther we go out into the space surrounding the magnet poles. Fig 31 gives a clear view of some of these lines. The spots which are marked N, S, are the places where the paper touches the ends or poles of the magnet, which is beneath the sheet of paper presenting the figure.

The iron filings, which are thrown on top of the sheet, arrange themselves in lines as seen. Between the poles these lines appear straight, and become more and more curved the longer the path becomes from one pole to the other. It must, however, be borne in mind that the sheet is but a single plane through the sphere or globe surrounding the magnet, and that the power of activity goes in all directions surrounding the poles, as the branches and leaves surround the trunk of a tree. These same curves of activity can be seen to go in all directions in space by taking a small compass needle and passing it from one pole to the other. The needle will during its travel change its position with relation to the two poles, and will always take such a position that its two ends lie in line with the particular curve which unites it with the two poles (Fig. 32). It is owing to this custom of representing this force by the

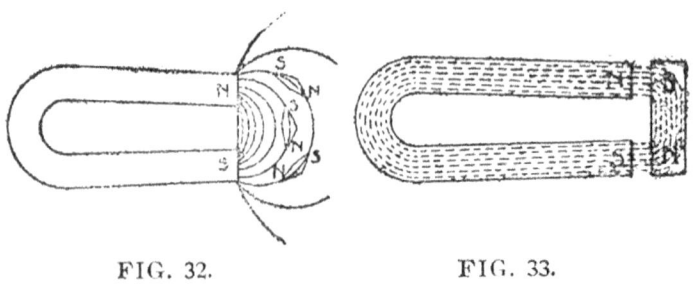

FIG. 32. FIG. 33.

curved lines that it became usual to speak of "magnetic lines of force," which, however, should not be considered as actual lines, nor that they simply connect the two poles, as in Figs. 24 and 25, but as a force which threads through the whole length of the magnet, as shown in Fig. 33. This energy is not only vested in the extremities or poles, but is the sum of the forces of all the particles of steel constituting the magnet. The energy is in the magnet, but its manifestations become apparent most strongly at the points where it passes from the magnetic medium to a non-magnetic one. Air is non-magnetic, while iron and steel

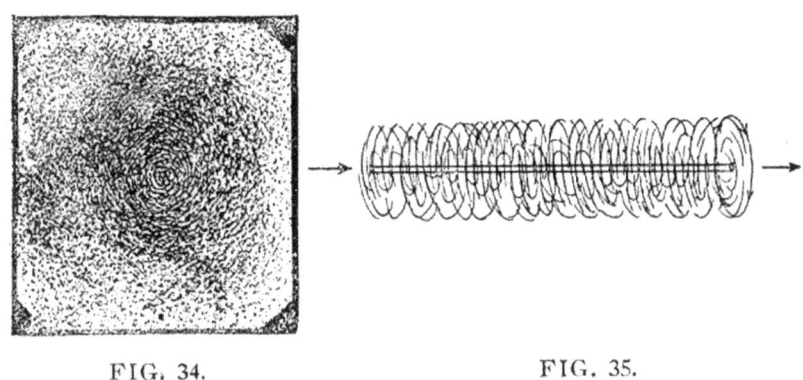

FIG. 34.   FIG. 35.

are strongly magnetic substances. Owing to the great preference that the magnetism has for iron, it selects the path indicated in Fig 33, rather than to go straight from the pole N to the S pole through the air. In passing through the iron the lines of magnetic force cause the armature or keeper to also become a magnet. The poles are marked S and N as abbreviations for "South" and "North," because they correspond to the poles or ends of the magnetic needle of a compass. The keeper becomes a magnet under the influence of the horseshoe magnet.

If we substitute for the keeper a permanent magnet, viz., a piece of steel in which the poles are fixed, we find that if the two magnets are faced N to S and S to N, as in this figure, they will attract each other. If placed so that the two N poles are together and the two S poles are together, no attraction will take place, but, on the contrary, they will repel each other, and from this fact comes the rule "like poles N, N, or S, S, repel each other, unlike poles attract each other."

A great step in advance was made when the following fact was discovered: It was found that if a wire carrying an electric current and a magnetic needle, delicately suspended, were brought close to each other, that the needle was deflected to one side. If the current flowed in a wire above the needle in the direction from south to north, namely, if the wire itself was held in a direction due north and south above the needle, and the current flowed north through the wire, then the north-seeking end of the needle was deflected to the west. If the wire was held above the needle, but turned round so that the current flowed from north to south, then the north-seeking point of the needle was deflected to the east. Lastly, if the wire was held below the needle, the direction of the deflection was reversed. It was clear, then, what had been long suspected, that there was some connection between magnetism and electricty.

This experiment also showed that the electric current could act through space, and acts on the magnetic needle just as the horseshoe magnet would. If that is the case

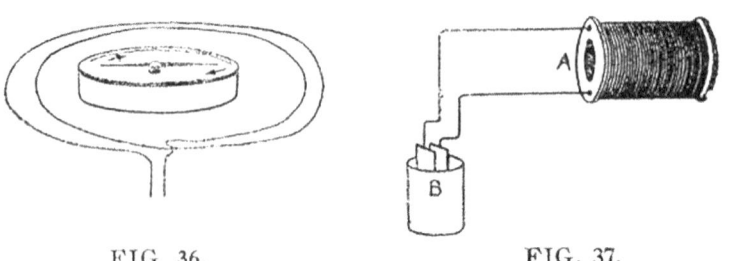

FIG. 36.   FIG. 37.

then it must disturb the space surrounding it while a current is flowing; it must establish a sphere around itself of the nature of a magnet, a sphere that has magnetic properties. Investigating the space around the wire with iron filings, we find a grouping of the little iron particles (Figs. 34 and 35), and that the wire carrying a current attracts iron filings. Fig 35 shows a picture of the force around the wire, while Fig. 34 shows an end view of Fig. 35.

Fig. 36 represents a magnetic needle surrounded by a coil of wire carrying a current. It appears that we have here the principle of an electric motor with this one difference, that owing to the arrangement of parts the movement is not rotary. Motion is imparted, but not continuous motion, in one direction. It was found further that if we take a spool of wire (Fig. 37) without any iron near it and send an electric current through it, as, for instance, from a battery B, through the coil A, that it behaved just

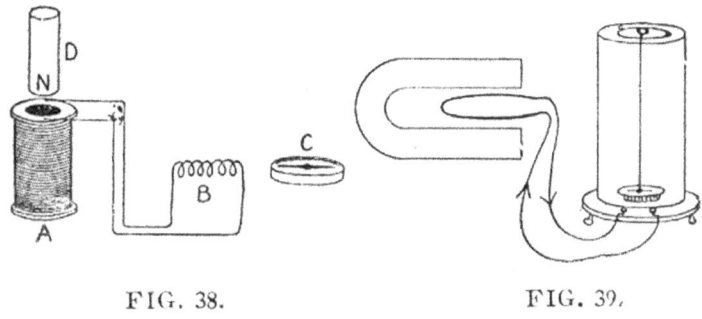

FIG. 38.   FIG. 39.

as a magnet would, viz., that it exhibited a north pole at one extremity and a south pole at the other, and that it attracted one end of the magnetic needle at one end and the other at the opposite end; just what we know would take place if we had an ordinary straight magnet or bar magnet instead of the spool with the current flowing through it.

Lastly, one more phenomenon must be mentioned, which will complete our picture. If we take a spool of wire A (Fig. 38) and connect it to another coil B several feet away, which is close to a magnetic needle C, and we approach a magnet D to the first coil A, then the needle is momentarily deflected. The needle C is far enough away not to be under the directing influence of the magnet D. What takes place is this: The sphere surrounding the magnet pole in its approach affects the coil A, and this disturbance in space is the cause of the flow of an electric current in coil A, which, passing through the coil B, disturbs the air surrounding it and changes it into a magnet, which in turn acts on the compass needle. Here we have one of the earliest transmissions of power to a distance.

Returning now to our simple magnet (Fig. 39), it will be clear and in accordance with facts that if a loop of wire, placed between the poles of a horseshoe magnet and connected to a delicate instrument for measuring electric currents, is turned between the poles of this magnet, such turn-

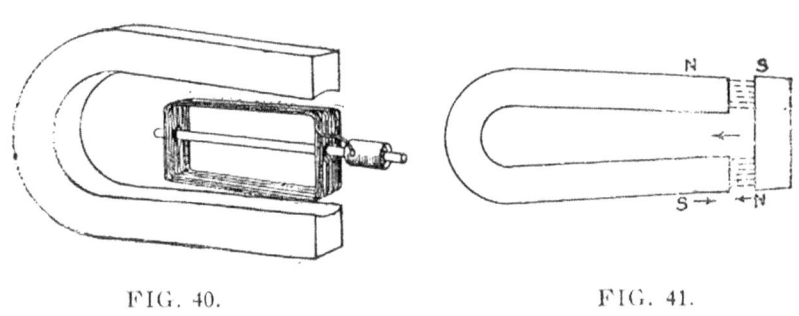

FIG. 40.   FIG. 41.

ing produces a temporary current which affects and deflects the needle of the instrument. An electric current is generated which flows from the loop to the instrument and back again, with the effect of deflecting the needle of the instrument. What has been found is that taking a magnet and turning a coil of wire in its sphere of activity, or (as it is called technically) in its magnetic field, an electric current is created or generated in this coil. The reader will now see that if this simple magnet, with the loop or a coil placed between its poles, is conveniently arranged on a shaft so as to turn it continually in the same direction (Fig. 40), a current will be produced that will last for some time instead of simply an impulse of current; this constitutes a dynamo in its simplest form. Of course such an arrangement gives but very weak currents and is not a commercial device, owing to its primitive mechanical arrangement, and also owing to the weakness of the permanent magnet, but this funda-

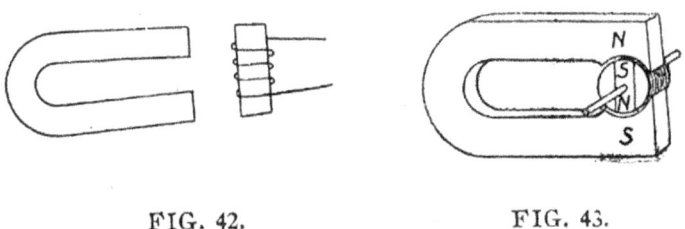

FIG. 42.   FIG. 43.

mental idea can be recognized in any and all of our modern macihnes.

Now let us start once more with our permanent magnet and go through the evolution until we reach the dynamo of to-day. Fig. 28 shows the permanent horseshoe magnet with its keeper in place. Fig. 41 shows the keeper or armature, as we will call it hereafter, some distance from the poles, with the field of activity in the space between the

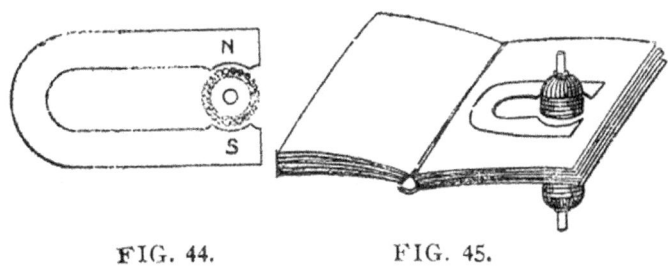

FIG. 44.   FIG. 45.

poles and the armature. The armature, under the influence of the magnet, becomes also a magnet and must exhibit poles, which are indicated by the letters N S, N S, in such a way that a south pole of the armature will stand before a north pole of the magnet. Under these conditions the force exerted causes mutual attraction between the magnet and its armature, resulting in a motion of the smaller piece, which moves toward the magnet, where all motion stops when it rests against the poles. If we now wind a coil around the armature, we would obtain a temporary current which lasts as long as the armature is approaching the poles (Fig. 42), but as soon as the armature comes to rest the current ceases. In a dynamo it is desired to produce currents continually, and therefore it is necessary to modify the form and relationship of the armature to the magnet. This is shown in Fig. 43. In this case the armature is

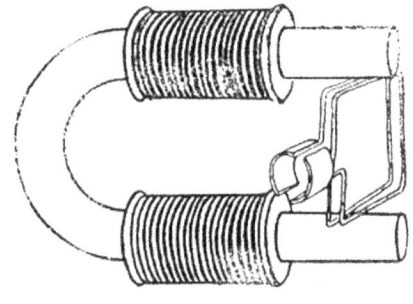

FIG. 46.

mounted on a spindle, a cylindrical piece of iron, which, magnetically considered, is a bar as in Fig. 41. Fig. 44 shows a magnet like Fig. 43, with the wires wound around the cylindrical armature core. The wires and the shaft are shown in section. The wire, which is to be rotated in the space of magnetic activity, is placed as near the poles as possible, as shown in section in Fig. 44. This figure is obtained by placing the magnet in the plane of the leaf or book (Fig. 45). The armature and wires lie at right angles, penetrating through all the leaves. If the armature in Fig. 45 be cut off, the end that projects on top is shown in Fig. 44. To collect the currents generated and bring them to devices, such as lamps or motors, we have to make some provision for collecting the electric current from the rotating armature to stationary points. This is done by connecting the ends of the rotating coils to metallic contact pieces or rings, which will be explained later.

To produce strong currents strong magnets are needed,

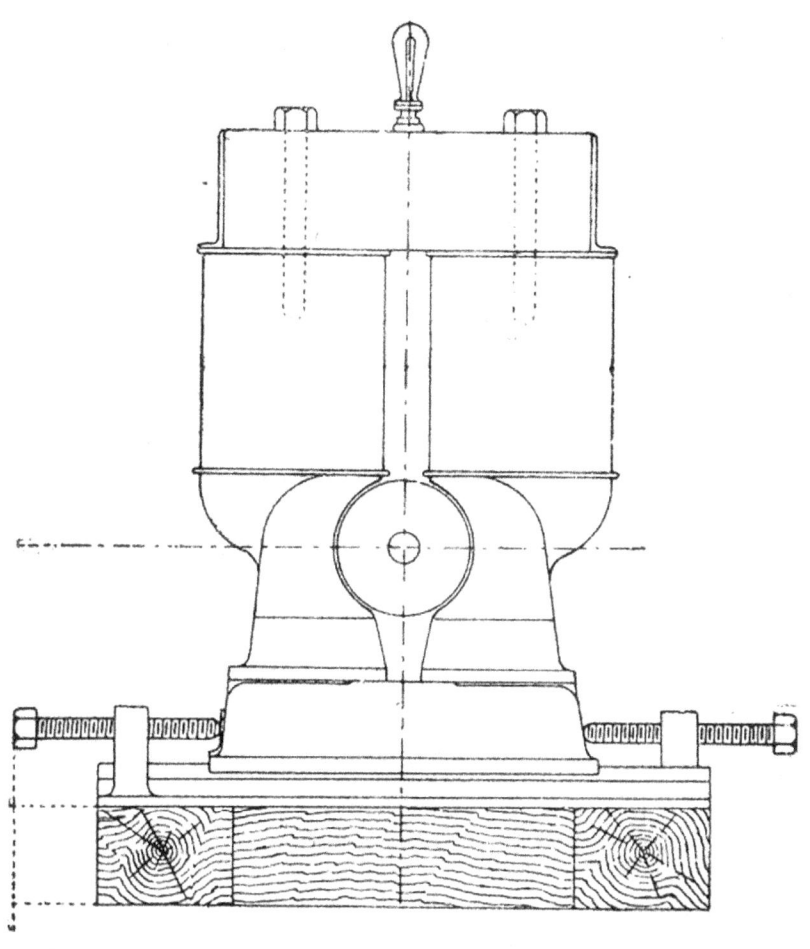

FIG. 47.

and it was found that permanent steel magnets were weakened when an armature with winding was made to generate heavy electric currents. It was further found that soft iron, when wound with coils through which a current was sent, became a far more powerful magnet than could be obtained in any other way. Therefore it became the practice to use wrought iron, cast iron or soft steel magnets for dynamos, and to magnetize them by a winding through which an electric current is sent as long as the machine is working. Fig. 46 shows our simple magnet provided with energizing coils, which, to distinguish them from the windings on the armature, are called the field magnet windings, or, in short, the field windings, because they belong to that magnet which establishes the field in which the other part or armature is

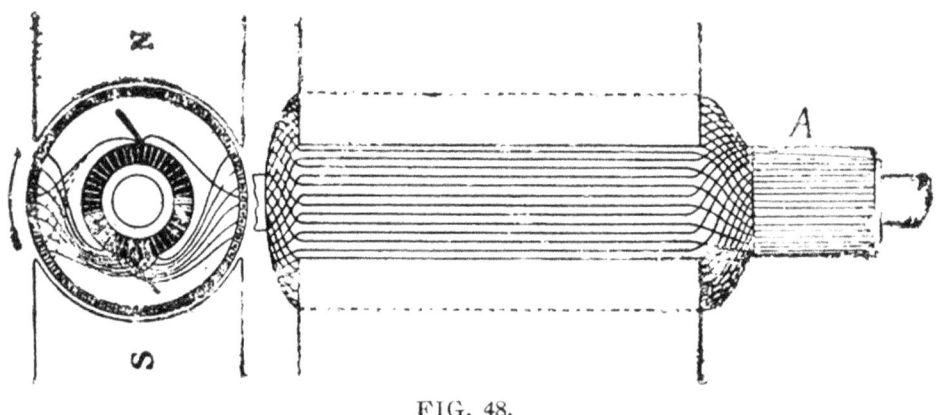

FIG. 48.

to rotate. Between the magnet poles is the armature with a winding and contact devices.

If we now compare the complete dynamo with the original magnet, we find that the only difference between them is that the dynamo is made more powerful than the magnet by the application of the coils, and the differences in the armatures are that the motion is changed from a lateral to a rotary one; further, that the armature is provided with a winding and a device for conveniently taking off the current generated by the rotating of the armature winding in the sphere of energy of the magnet. The reader will now clearly see that there is no frictional contact required between the armature and the field magnet, an erroneous view so frequently expressed by people not conversant with the subject.

We are now prepared to look critically at any kind of a dynamo, from the simplest and weakest to the largest machines built to-day, without confusion and without the idea of great complication as regards the nature of its operation, for now the single magnet with the single loop between the poles will be ever present before the mental eye.

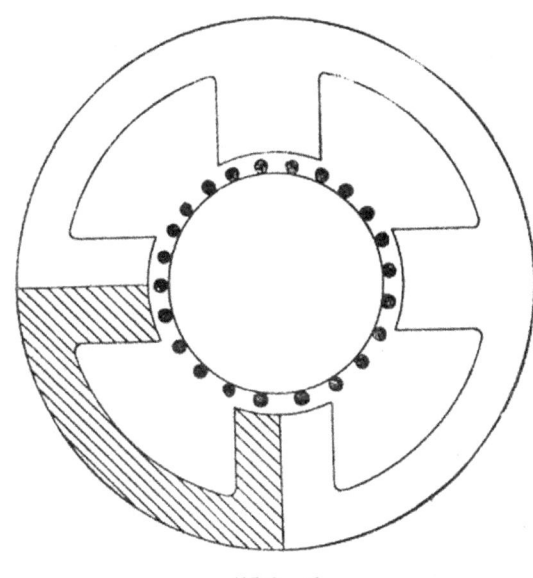

FIG. 49.

Let us examine in this way a few of the types of dynamos used in every-day practice. Fig. 47 shows the outline of an Edison dynamo, one of the older types, still in use in some stations. The horseshoe magnet with its windings will readily be recognized in this machine. It is built with its poles downward and its armature between the poles, which are extended so as to surround the armature. Fig. 48 shows a front and side view of the armature, the iron core being completely covered by the wire. On the right side may be seen the contact terminals, called the commutator, which is marked A. In Fig. 25 was shown a large railway generator capable of driving a great many cars. Fig. 49 is a skeleton of a multipolar field magnet, which shows a magnet with four poles and consists of four horseshoe magnets, one of which is shown shaded. The armature is shown located between the poles.

This elementary description, explaining the nature of the generation of an electric current, shows clearly how simple is the principle underlying an electric machine. It is a magnet at rest, combined with a rotating piece of iron wrapped with wire, that constitutes a dynamo; and furthermore, a machine that is used as a dynamo may also be used as a motor. The name dynamo or motor changes with the service to be rendered. If the machine sown in Fig. 47 be driven by a steam engine, and is supplying electric current. it is a dynamo; if, however, an electric current is applied to it, and it does mechanical work, it is a motor. These differences should be clear in the mind of the reader. If there are parts he does not understand clearly, he should discuss the subject with such persons of his acquaintance who are competent to explain the matter to him.

CHAPTER II.

THE ELECTRIC RAILWAY MOTOR AND CAR EQUIPMENT.

We are now ready to look into the details of an electric railway motor. In Chapter I were explained the principles on which all dynamos and motors are built. We found a motor to be simply a magnet in which the magnetism is produced by the electric current, and in which one part, called an armature, is caused to revolve by magnetic attraction between it and the poles of other parts, called the field magnets. We have also learned how the electric current is transmitted through wires, and what precautions are necessary to insulate or confine it to the proper wires or conductors.

Let us go more into the details of the internal working of the armature of the dynamo or motor, and show the reason why in one case large engines are used to produce the electric current, and while at other times the armature will turn itself and give out energy. In Fig. 48 is shown an armature complete. It consists of a shaft on which is mounted an iron core closely wrapped with wire, and the ends of the wire coils are connected to the contact terminals, called the commutator, on which the brushes rest to collect the current. An armature is represented in diagram in Fig. 50. The iron armature core A is shown in form of a ring. The winding B is uniformly wrapped around the core, and every three turns a wire is led to the commutator C, which is divided into eight parts because the winding shows eight coils. The number of coils varies on different kinds of armatures.

The commutator consists of copper bars insulated from one another by mica. These bars form the ends of the armature coils. They are made heavier than the wires so as to last a long time, being exposed to wear by rubbing contact, and to be detachable when worn out. On the commutator rest the brushes D, D1. If the armature is traversed by a current entering at brush D, as for instance when it is used as a motor, the current passes to segment 1, and from there through connecting wire a to the armature wire proper. Here it has a double pass, as shown by the arrows.

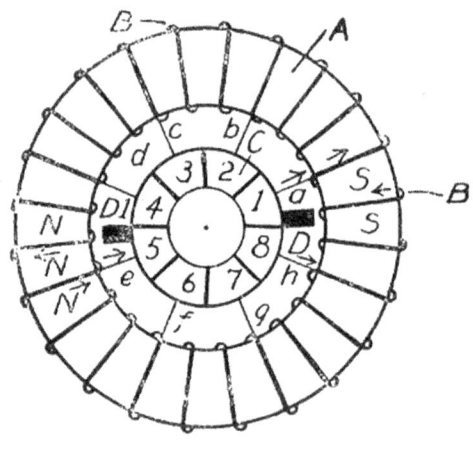

FIG. 50.

Half the current will follow the direction indicated by the arrows on the upper half of the ring, and the other part of the current will follow the wires wound on the lower half of the armature core. The two currents unite again wire e, enter segment 5 brush D1, and leave the armature. This flow takes place in whatever position the armature may be. For instance, assuming the brushes D, D1 stationary and the armature turning; if the armature has turned so far around that segment 2 would be under the brush D, then segment 6 would be under brush D1. The current would go to the armature winding through b and leave it by way of f. In this way each one of the segments and connecting wires has to perform in succession its work. The current in going around the core makes a magnet out of the iron, as indicated by the letters N, S.

For the sake of convenience in understanding, the armature core may be also considered divided into two half rings, as in Fig. 51, the upper and lower; then the current flowing around the upper half makes it a magnet, and similarly the

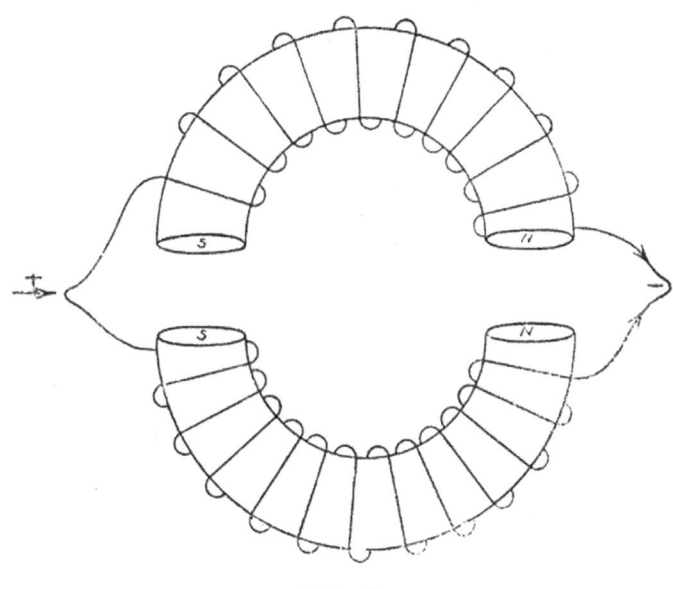

FIG. 51.

current in the lower half will make that half become a magnet. The poles are marked N and S. The poles caused by each half of the current are indicated on the ring. An N pole on one side and an S pole on the opposite side in each half is produced, and both together make again one N pole and one S pole, but of double the strength. As long as the brushes stand in this position the magnetic poles will stay in space in the same position, however much the armature may rotate, because just as many turns are leaving the brush on one side as are brought under it from the opposite side.

The iron ring wrapped with the armature wire represents in reality two half circular magnets butting together with similar poles. Whether these are curved as is Fig. 51, or have another form, for instance, being straight bar magnets, does not alter anything in the nature of the armature. Nor is there, as far as principle is concerned, any difference between a ring armature, shown in Fig. 50, and a drum armature. An armature made for a street railway motor is generally made of thin discs mounted in a compact way on a shaft, (Fig. 52). The wire in this case has to be all applied externally. It cannot be threaded through the center

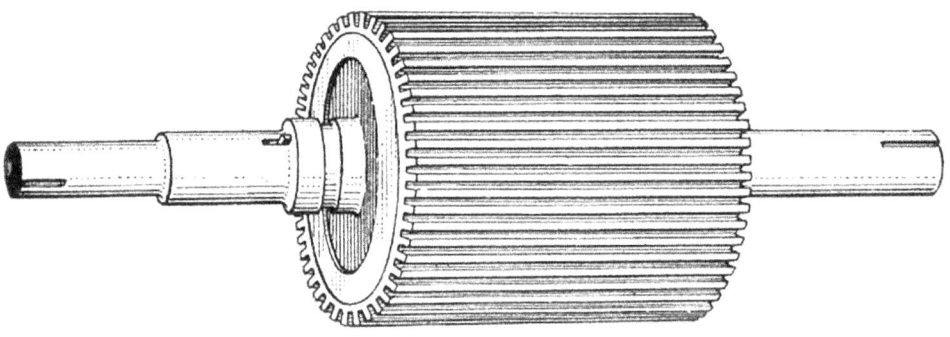

FIG. 52.

as in Fig. 50, but the results is the same. Fig. 53 is a diagram indicating a railway motor with an iron core made of discs and the magnetizing copper wire wound all around the surface.

The diagram represents the armature in section. Now suppose the brushes to be set as they are in Fig. 50, then the current flowing in the coils with which the armature core is wound will cause N and S poles in the armature as indicated. Current is also sent through the coils on the field magnets, causing N and S poles in the magnet as indicated. It will be evident that the S pole of the armature will endeavor to place itself in front of the N pole of the field magnet, being attracted by it and at the same time repelled by the S pole near it. Similarly the N pole of the armature will try to get in front of the S field pole, being attracted by this pole and repelled by the N pole; but as the brushes are stationary, the magnetic poles S, N of the armature remain fixed in space between the poles, while the conductors carrying the current and the core on which they are wound are turning in the direction of the arrow as long as a current is conducted into the armature.

In a motor, therefore, the electrical energy furnished by some outside source causes rotation capable of developing mechanical energy. In a dynamo it is just the opposite. There is no electrical energy given; it has to be produced.

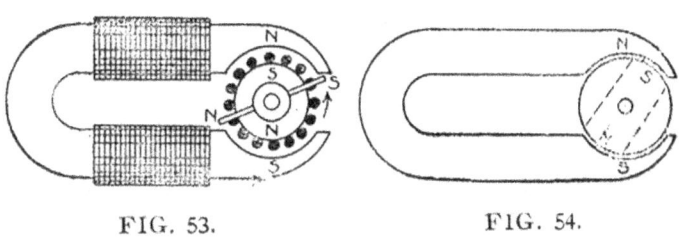

FIG. 53.   FIG. 54.

The wire coils passing in front of the magnet poles generate current.

Fig. 54 illustrates this action. The field magnet N S changes the armature into a magnet with the poles as indicated, the S pole of the armature approximately facing the N pole of the field and the N pole of the armature nearly facing the S pole of the field magnet. There exists mutual attraction between the armature and the field magnet. To generate a current, the armature must be turned between the energized field magnet poles, which is equivalent to attempting the pulling away the armature poles from under the field poles. This we know from the first experimnent mentioned in the book means the expenditure of energy.

We can now look more intelligently at the parts of a

modern electric railway motor than we could when we first went through the shops. We have already seen the external parts of a motor in Chapter 1, Part 1, Figs. 7 to 16. From the foregoing explanations we are now in a position to examine the various internal parts of an electric motor. Fig.

FIG. 55.

55 shows a railway motor with its frame opened, giving a view of its interior parts. The armature, A, is mounted upon a shaft and at one end of the armature is the commutator C, consisting of a cylinder of insulated copper bars, to which the ends of the armature coils are connected. Surrounding the armature are four field magnets, or poles, P, around which are wound coil of wire to magnetize them for

the purpose previously explained. The brushes, B, conduct the current to and from the armature through their contact with the commutator. These brushes consist of carbon blocks which are held in brush holders and which are pressed against the commutator by springs. The path of the current through the motor is as follows: Starting at one of the brushes the current passes through all the coils of wire upon the armature, beginning at whatever commutator bar the brush happens to rest upon, and comes out upon another commutator bar under the second brush. From this brush the current is led through all the field coils wound around the poles surrounding the armature, and this completes the circuit through the motor. With the current flowing through both the armature and the field coils, both the armature and the field become magnets, and each attracts the other in such a way as to cause the armature to turn as previously explained. To reverse the direction in which the armature revolves, which reverses the direction of the car, it is only necessary to change the direction in which the current flows through the armature, allowing the current to flow through the fields in the same direction as before, or we can also reverse the direction of revolution by permitting the current to flow in the same direction through the armature and reversing its direction through the field coils. If the armature current is reversed the magnetism in the armature is reversed, the north pole becoming a south pole and the south pole a north pole. In order to reverse the current in the armature the wires from the armature brushes are led to the controller independently from the terminals of the field coils, so that the connections of the armature terminals can be reversed at the controller when it is desired to reverse the direction of rotation of the motor. For this reason there will always be at least four wires leading out from the motor.

We will now trace the electrical circuit through the car. The current, as we know, comes from the power house through the feed wires and trolley wire, and flows through the trolley wheel down the trolley pole to the trolley base. This base is insulated from the ground by the wood which forms the car body. From the trolley base a wire conducts the current to the canopy switch over one platform, and passing through this switch it flows through another wire to the canopy switch over the other platform and from there a

FIG. 56.

wire generally concealed in a corner post of the car carries the current to the car fuse box, mentioned in Chapter 1, Part 1. The canopy switch, Fig. 56, is also sometimes called the main motor switch, the overhead switch or the auxiliary switch. These switches are generally provided with what is known as a blow-out magnet coil, for the purpose of blowing out the arc when the switch is opened. The next piece of apparatus in the circuit is the fuse box, which is a device for protecting the motors from an excessive flow of current.

All the current flowing through the car motors passes through this fuse box, of which there are several styles on the market. The simplest fuse consists merely of a piece

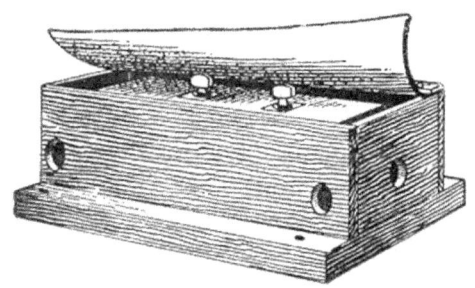

FIG. 57.

of soft wire generally made of some alloy of lead having a low current carrying capacity. This piece of fuse wire will melt and open the electric circuit whenever the current flows through the motors of such an amount as might burn the cotton insulation on the coils of the armature or the field

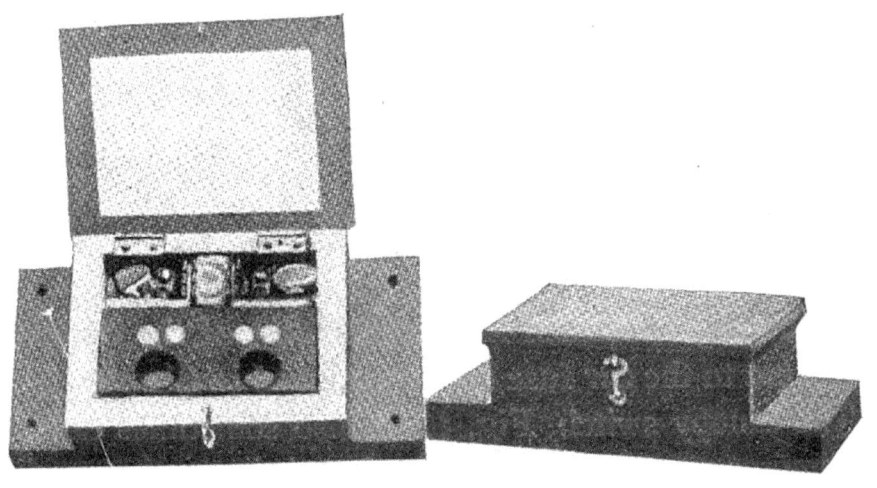

FIG. 58.

magnet. When too much current is permitted to flow through any wire it becomes heated and the greater the amount of current the hotter the wire becomes. If, therefore, something should happen on the car to allow too much current to flow through the motors, the wire upon their armatures and fields would become heated so as to burn the insulation upon them, and would eventually be melted if the circuit were not protected with a fuse which would melt when the current exceeded a certain predetermined amount. The fuse is frequently a short length of metal connected between two binding posts, and of a material that will melt at a very low temperature, although sometimes a small copper wire is used. When copper is used it must be of a size much

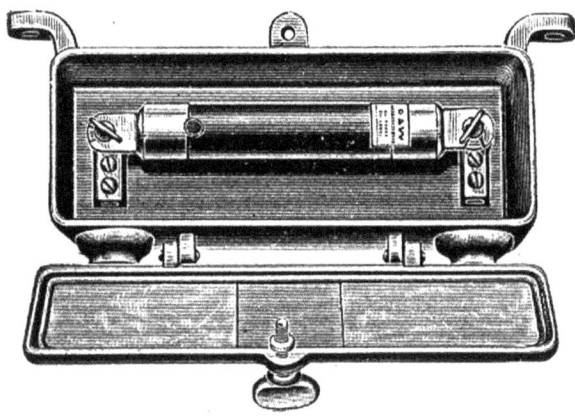

FIG. 59.

smaller than any of the other wires on the car, so that it will melt before any other of the wires in the circuit can get dangerously hot.

The Westinghouse Company employs a fuse which has to be taken out of the box with its supporting blocks before it can be renewed (Fig. 58), but with this exception the usual fuse box consists simply of two terminals fixed inside the fuse box between which the fuse is clamped, as in the General Electric fuse box (Fig. 57).

In addition to the bare wire fuses described above, there are various covered fuses such as the D. E. W. fuse, Fig. 59, and the Noark fuse, Fig. 60. The latter has a fusible conductor which is enclosed in a tube and around the conductor is a special filling which prevents any arc or flash under short circuits. A fuse of this kind is a great improvement over the old-fashioned bare wire fuses, as they do not blow with the loud report and heavy flash which accompany the blowing of a bare fuse. They are also of advantage in not blistering the varnish and paint of the car, which frequently happens with the uncovered fuse. An-

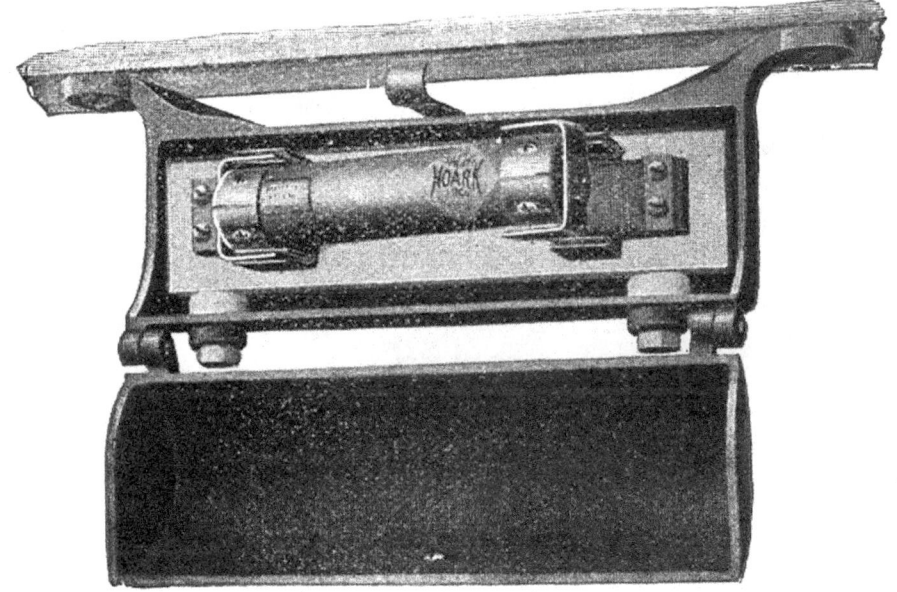

FIG. 60.

other advantage of these fuses is that they are inserted in the fuse box by simply pushing the tube into its seat between clamping springs, and there are no thumb screws to be manipulated, which is a difficult matter in severe weather.

Automatic circuit breakers have recently been used to a large extent to take the place of the fuse, and they are preferable to fuses for a number of reasons, the chief of which are that they may be arranged to break the circuit when the current exceeds any predetermined amount with much more accuracy than a wire fuse, and they are thrown into circuit again simply by the movement of a handle without the necessity of replacing any of the parts, as with the fuse. There are a number of circuit breakers on the market, one of which, called the I. T. E. circuit breaker, is shown in Fig. 61, but they are all designed practically upon the same principle. The principal parts of the automatic circuit breaker are a switch which closes against a spring, and which is held in its closed position by means of a trip. In the circuit of the machine is placed a magnetic coil, the function of which is

FIG. 61.

to attract an armature whose movement releases the trip, permitting the spring to throw the contact surfaces apart and break the circuit. The cause of the armature being attracted and the trip released is that the magnet coil is wound so that with a normal amount of current the magnet is not strong enough to attract the armature, but the moment an excessive amount of current is used the strength of the magnet is correspondingly increased, so that the armature is attracted and the trip released, which opens the circuit.

The next device on the car to which the current is led is the lightning arrester. This is a device to deflect lightning or atmospheric discharges from the circuit to the ground before they have an opportunity to reach the motors or other electrical apparatus on the car. There is a strong tendency for a lightning discharge to take the shortest and most direct path to the ground, and it will readily arch over a small gap or air space or will pierce through insulating materials to the ground. If it were not for the lightning arrester, the

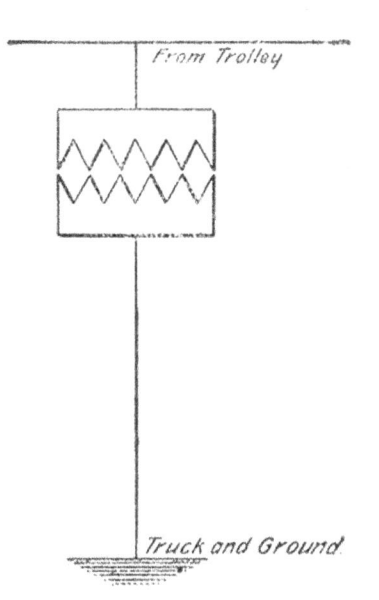

FIG. 62.

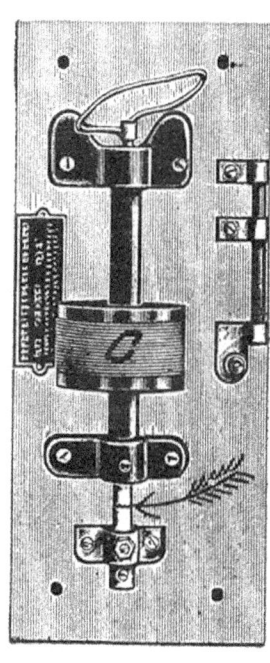

FIG. 63.

lightning would frequently jump through the insulation of the armatures or field magnets of the car motor, and while the very small current of the lightning discharge would do no harm of itself, the arc which it would establish in jumping to the ground would be followed up by the line current from the station, which would burn out the windings immediately. The tendency of lightning to jump to the ground by the shortest path is the principle upon which most all lightning arresters are designed. These devices usually consist of some arrangement whereby the lightning can easily pass down the wire across to the ground by jumping between points set a small fraction of an inch apart. Various provisions are made by different manufacturers to prevent the current from the power house from following the lightning when it is deflected to earth. Fig. 62 shows a diagram of the connections of the lightning arrester. One terminal is connected to the wire from the trolley and the other to the motor truck and therefore to the ground. The lightning jumps across between the points and is thus led to the earth. Fig. 63 shows a Garton arrester. In it may be seen the two carbon points indicated by an arrow between which the

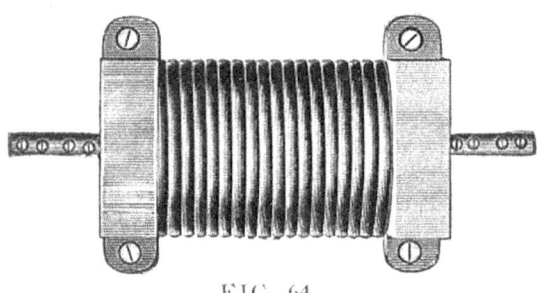

FIG. 64.

lightning jumps on its way to earth. In order to break this special circuit after the lightning has passed so that the current from the dynamo cannot follow by the same path that is taken by the lightning to earth, the circuit to the lightning arrester is automatically broken by an electro magnet which pulls the two carbons apart as soon as current flows through the coil C. It will be seen that the circuit of the lightning arrester or by-pass is constantly open except when temporarily closed, as the lightning flash crosses it, and even then it is a circuit of very high resistance. It is therefore clear that while the lightning arrester is connected to the trolley wire, yet no current from the trolley line goes through it. A kicking coil, Fig. 64, is used in connection with the lightning arrested, and an inductive resistance such as this coil is the only resistance that offers hindrance to the passage of static electricity or lightning. The kicking coil is put in the circuit immediately after the lightning arrester and its inductive resistance tends to drive the discharge through the arrester before it reaches the motors or other apparatus. Fig. 65 shows the Wurtz non-arcing lightning arrester with the outside cover removed. The principle upon which this arrester is based is that a discharge will pass over a non-con-

FIG. 65.   FIG. 66.

ducting surface, such as wood, more readily than through an equal air gap, and the discharge will take place still more readily if a pencil or carbon mark be drawn over the non-conducting surface. In order to maintain a dynamo arc, fumes or vapors of the electrodes must be present. The instrument is constructed with two metal electrodes mounted upon a block of hard wood with charred or carbonized grooves upon it to provide a path for the discharge. Another block of wood is fastened closely upon the first block, entirely covering the grooves and electrodes. The discharge takes place over the charred grooves which provide an easy path for it, and as there is no room for vapor between the tightly fitting blocks no arc can be formed. Fig. 66 shows the General Electric type of lightning arrester for trolley cars.

After the line current has passed the point where the lightning arrester is connected, it flows through what is called the kicking coil previously mentioned. The object of this is to aid in making it difficult for the lightning to flow toward the motors, owing to an inductive kick in the spiral winding, and to increase the liability of its going to ground through the lightning arrester.

After leaving the choke coil the current enters one of the many wires conveniently held by a hose. This wire is connected to both car controllers. A number of other wires lead from each controller to motors and regulating resistance. After leaving the motors the current flows to a wire which is securely fastened to the iron or frame of the motor, from which the circuit continues through the various motor supports to the car truck and car axle, then to the wheel rims through the rails back to the generator. Next in importance to the motors are the car controllers. As the motorman has chiefly to do with the controllers they will be treated in a subsequent chapter.

CHAPTER III.

CONTROLLERS.

For controlling the speed of electric cars three general methods have been employed, two of which, however, are practically obsolete to-day. One method is by means of a rheostat, which was the system adopted by the Thomson-Houston Co. In the Thomson-Houston method of control the motors are connected permanently in parallel, and the rheostat is inserted in series with the two motors, and contains sufficient resistance to reduce the starting pressure to less than half of the total voltage. This resistance is gradually cut out until the full voltage of the circuit passes through the motors when the car reaches its maximum speed. There are two types of rheostats made by the Thomson-Houston Co. known as type D-51 and D-81. The former is semi-circular in shape, and the latter is round. Another method of motor control for street cars is that of the Sprague system in which the field coils are divided into several sections, the sections being connected in series and also in series with the armature in starting the car, and changing by successive steps of the controller until they are all in parallel, and in parallel with the armature, when the car attains its maximum speed. A starting rheostat is also used with this method of control, but is in series only on the first notch of the controller when the car is starting from rest. Both of these systems are now practically out of use, and can only be found on cars equipped many years ago, but as they are liable to be met with on some of the older roads, a short reference and description of them has been included. Of these two systems the Sprague system is the most economical in the use of current, but owing to the complication of the windings, is more liable to derangements and burn outs. With the straight rheostatic method there is no change whatever in the connections of the motor fields, and while this method is less efficient than the other, its freedom from accidents and burn outs is a distinct advantage.

The series parallel method of control which is now universally used, and which has supplanted all other methods, consists in grouping the motors on the car, together with the starting rheostat, in series and gradually, through the successive steps of the controller, changing them to parallel connection when the car attains its greatest speed. A large number of controllers of both the General Electric, Westinghouse and other makes, are described in the following pages. It may be stated, however, that the type K General Electric controllers, are the ones most commonly used.

The car controller is a combination of switches adapted to control the speed of the motors by admitting more or less electrical energy to the motors as the case may require. These changes of connections may be made by a number of independent and separate switches, but if this were done many switches would be required, and they would be slow and awkward to operate and would occupy too much room. Experience has shown that a circular contact drum is the quickest acting and most suitable device on which a great many changes of connections can be made simply and easily. The purpose of the controller is threefold:

1. To connect the motors into the circuit so that current can flow through them.
2. To regulate the amount of current flowing to the mo-

tors so as to make a gradual start and control the speed of the car.

3. To govern the direction of travel of the car.

The electrical pressure on the trolley line (technically called voltage) is kept practically constant at the power house. Therefore, if the current at full pressure were admitted suddenly to the motors, and no means provided to allow it to rise gradually, we would have to expect a similar abrupt and sudden start by the motors from a state of rest. Admitting the full current would be a strain on the electrical parts, and similarly the sudden start from rest to high speed would tax the bearings and other mechanical supports and gears, to say nothing of the discomfort which the passengers would experience by the jerk with which the motors would start the car.

To control the amount of current flowing to the motor it is necessary to consume a portion of the pressure under which the current flows by interposing some material which offers a resistance to the flow of the current until the motor has been gradually increased to its normal speed. All the switches or contacts for such grading or varying of resistance are mounted on the drum of the controller, while the resistance itself is generally fixed at a convenient place below the car body. Substances that offer resistance to the flow of current are iron wire, iron strips or plates, german silver, etc. For street railway purposes iron plates or bands are generally used, which are supported in an iron frame, the turns or convolutions being insulated from each other and the fire proof frame by mica. The complete device is termed a resistance, though some call it rheostat or diverter. Let us assume, for the sake of illustration, that the total length of the iron resistance band is 40 ft. in divisions of 10 ft. each, these divisions being connected to the controller terminals by means of wires mentioned in the previous chapter. If now this controller were placed on the first notch, the whole 40 ft. of iron band would be in circuit with the motor, and the pressure that could reach the motor reduced just the amount that would be lost in the 40 ft. of iron band. Turning the controller to the second notch, 10 ft. of this iron band would be cut out so that but 30 ft. would be in circuit. The pressure that could reach the motor in this case would, of course, be greater and its speed would increase. Turning the controller to the third notch, but 20 ft.; to the fourth notch, but 10 ft. of the resistance would be left in the

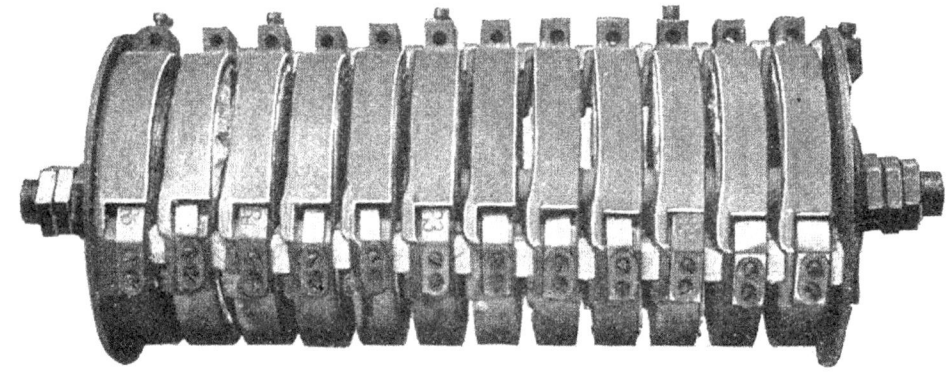

FIG. 67.

circuit, and at the fifth position the resistance would be out entirely, causing an increase of speed with every reduction in resistance and a maximum speed when all resistance was cut out.

A Westinghouse resistance or diverter is shown in Fig. 67. Its terminals (by which as just explained the resistance is subdivided) are led to the controller. In order to clearly understand all the different changes and conditions that take place by means of the controllers, it is desirable to make the reader acquainted first with the different modes of circuit connection and their names, and then immediately apply them to standard types of controllers. After the preliminary explanation one type of each make in general use will be described in detail, and the rest will be understood after a simple statement of the successive steps and changes as they take place.

If several parts or conductors are grouped so that the total current flows in succession through all parts, they are said to be grouped in "series," as for instance in Fig. 68.

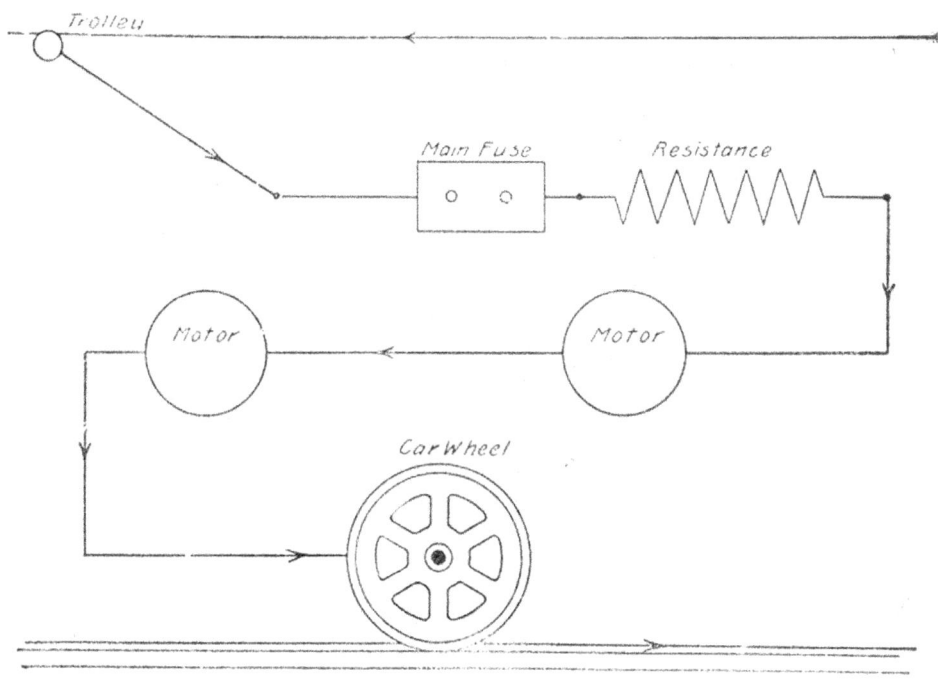

FIG. 68.

The trolley, the main fuse and the resistance carry the total current that goes to the motors, and they are said, or each one of them is said, to be in series with the motors. The motors are also in series with each other, as the current flows first through one, then through the other. It will be clear that if for any cause the main fuse would melt, there would be a separation between the trolley pole and the resistance and the current could not flow.

Another mode of connection is called "parallel" or "multiple" connection. This is shown in Fig. 69. The full current supplied to a car goes down the trolley pole, and if the motors are grouped, as shown in this figure, the current will divide and half of it will go to one motor and the other half to the other motor. Where the circuits of the motors are connected again the two currents join and flow on as

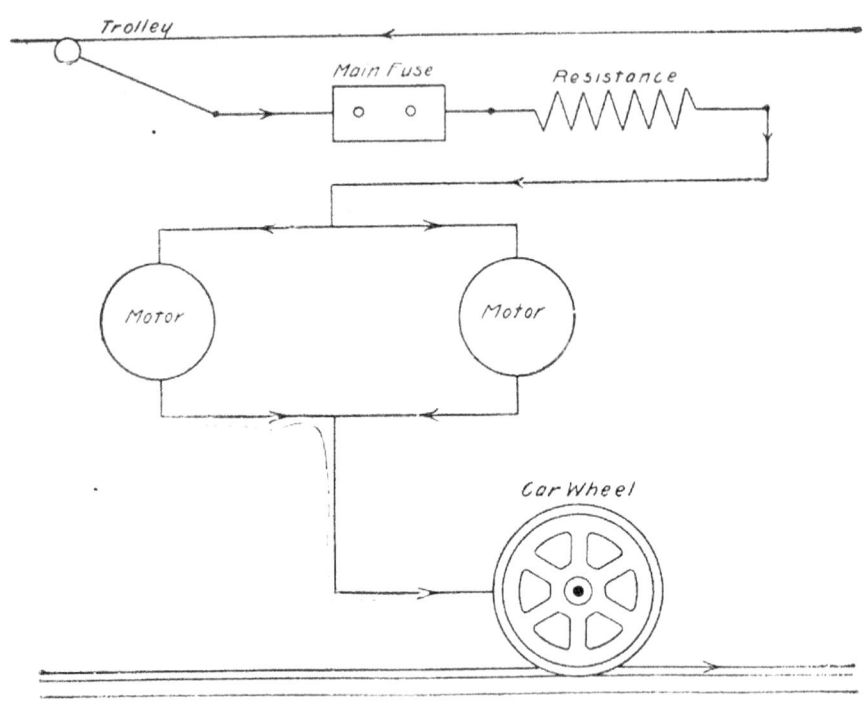

FIG. 69.

one through the car wheel and rail. The two motors are connected in parallel or multiple with one another. However, this connection is not restricted to motors only. Any two or more conductors placed in such a relation that the original current will split up into several paths and join at a place further on, are called connected in parallel, or shunt, or in multiple. For instance, resistance may be in parallel with or in shunt circuit to the field coils of a motor (Fig. 70), a connection which is made in some modern controllers.

A third way of connecting parts is made by a combination of the two above ways. Some of the devices with relation to others are in series with one another and in parallel with others, and such grouping is called series-parallel or parallel-series connection, Fig. 71 explaining this clearly. It represents a condition of grouping of motors on large electric locomotives. There are shown four motors, 1, 2, 3 and 4.

Evidently the current splits at A, divides into two currents, one of which flows through motors 1 and 2, the other through motors 3 and 4. The volume of current that goes

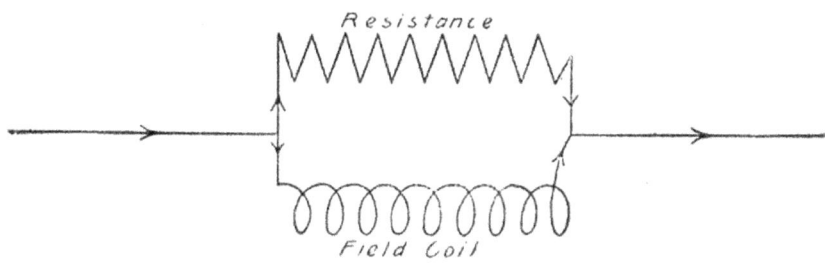

FIG. 70.

through motor 2 must therefore be the same as that going through motor 1, and the relation is similar between motors 3 and 4. At point B the currents join and the total current flows to the car axle and car wheel C. In this combination motors 1 and 2 are in series, and so are motors 3 and 4, but the 1 and 2 combined are in parallel connection to 3 and 4 combined, and the whole combination is called series-parallel.

Returning now to the controllers themselves, the old style (some being still in use) installed up to 1893 consisted of a drum with contacts mounted thereon which were the terminals for trolley, motor armature, motor field, resistance and ground. The handle or lever when turned to the left caused the car to go ahead, when turned to the right caused it to go backward. The handle was in the "off" position (meaning that circuit was open and the current turned off from the motors) when it stood centrally on the controller and nearest to the motorman or operator. This condition existed in the controllers of the Sprague, Edison, Westinghouse, Wightman and Steel Motor companies.

The old Thomson-Houston motor has no such cylinder

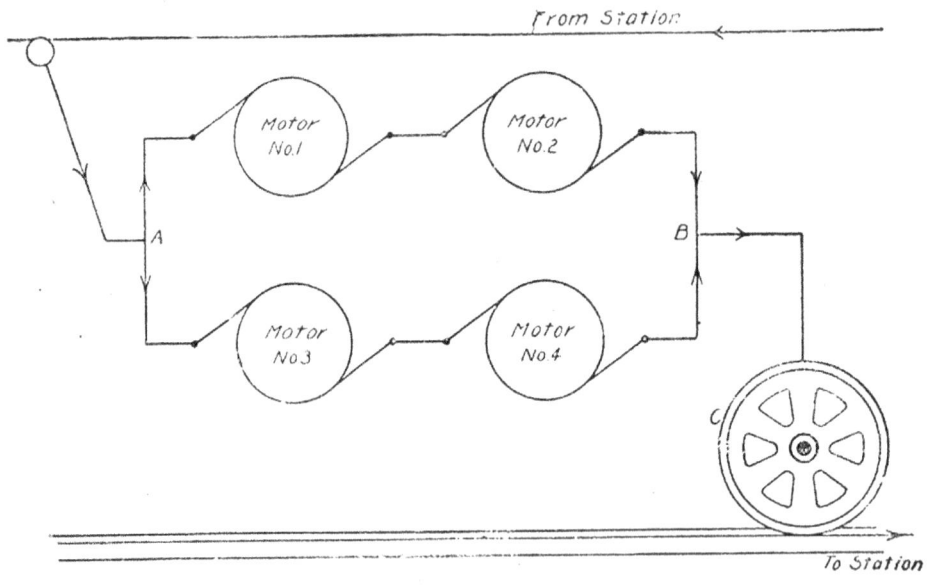

FIG. 71.

controller, but instead two brass handles which turn rods extending below the car, where one moves an arm over a sheet iron resistance (see Fig. 72) for gradually cutting out more and more of the resistance, and the other handle operated a reversing switch which caused the current to flow through the motor so as to reverse the direction of rotation of the armatures. This latter handle, placed in the forward position, causes the car to go forward, and when pulled as far back as possible the car moves back. The upper handle or controller handle is moved always in the same direction. The reversing handle should never be moved unless the other handle is in the "off" position. The connections made by this controller or rheostat are indicated by the diagram, Fig. 73. Let A represent the trolley wire, B the trolley pole, C a contact arm, R the rheostat or resistance of sheet iron in zig-zag shape, the circles M, M indicating the motors and G the wheel on the rail H. On the "off" piston the contact C is not in touch with resistance R, there-

FIG. 72.

fore no current will leave the trolley wire. The lever C makes contact with resistance R, and cuts it out gradually until lever C is brought around to the "on" position, when no current flows through the resistance, but passes directly from the end of the contact arm to the motors, where it divides, half going to one motor and half to the other.

In car equipments installed in early days, the connections between controllers and motors were such that the motors were permanently grouped in parallel with one another. The controllers operating these equipments are known as parallel controllers. One sometimes met with on older roads is the Westinghouse parallel controller known as type D. Projecting through the cover plate of this controller is the spindle on which the operating handle is placed. This spindle carries the centrally located cylinder with its ten contact cylinder bands. Above this cylinder or drum is located a ratchet wheel having large teeth, and as many notches as there are

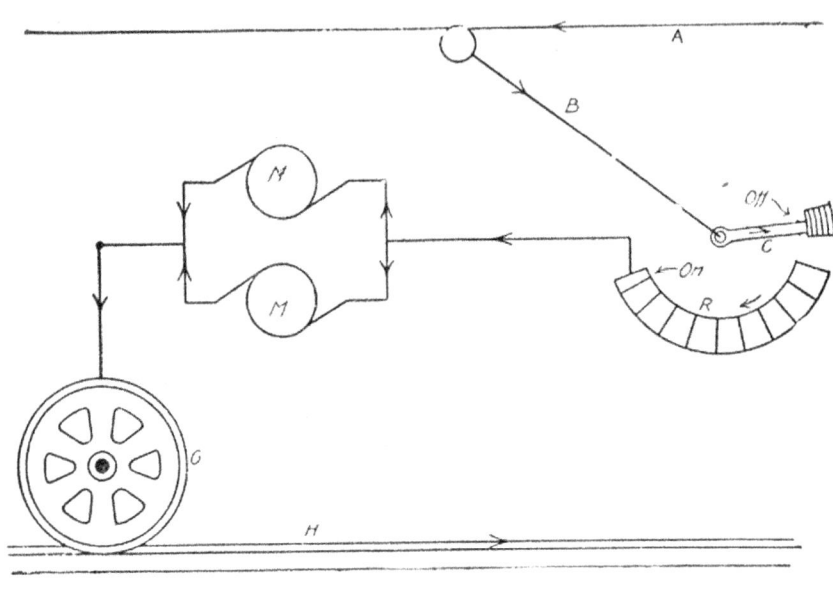

FIG. 73.

positions for the handle or changes of electrical connections and speeds. In this ratchet wheel fits a small roller held in an arm and receiving tension by a spring. By means of this contrivance it is possible to bring the controller always into the same position for each point, and without having to look at the handle to be sure that it is exactly on a notch.

On the sides of the drum are contact fingers, and below the drum are a number of contact blocks provided with screws into which the trolley wire, ground wire and others are attached which connect to the resistance or diverter and motors. The circular contacts on the drum are not of the same length; the largest ones are the four on the upper end of the drum and the lowest one. These are of equal length and on turning the drum in one direction or the other, these five connections are established at the same time. In this first position, the motors are connected with trolley and ground and the whole resistance is in circuit with the two motors which are permanently in parallel. The remaining five circular contact pieces are of different length. The largest of them is the second from the bottom and the smallest is the sixth from the bottom. These middle contacts have the purpose of cutting out portions of the different resistance from the motor circuit. When the controller handle is moved to the second notch a part of the resistance is removed from activity by the second contact from the bottom. Turning the drum to notch 3, the third segment from the bottom of the drum further reduces the resistance. Continuing by turning the handle to notch 4 another part of the resistance is cut out and sending the handle to notch 5, the last part of the resistance is cut out of the motor circuit by the smallest circular contact. At this position the motors receive the full pressure and have their greatest speed.

When the car is at rest the controller handle stands straight back. To start take hold of it with the left hand and push it to the left in the direction of the hands of the watch, until at the fifth position, it meets a raised part on the controller cover beyond which the handle cannot pass. Turning the handle as described will send the car ahead. To back up the car or to run it backward, the handle is turned from the "off" position or (position of rest when car is standing still) to the right. To the right, there are the same number of notches and speeds; the only difference is that the direction of car travel is reversed.

Since 1893 an improved form of controller, called the

series-parallel controller, has come into general use. The power required when first starting a car with the motors in series is only one-fourth what it would be with the same motors in parallel as on the old controllers just described. Consequently in the modern controller the motors are in series as in Fig. 68, on the first few points of the controller, and after about half speed has been reached they are connected in parallel as in Fig. 69. Hence the name, series-parallel controller.

The difference between the old method and the new is that formerly, to reduce the pressure at the motor terminals at the start, a great resistance was inserted to consume a part of the pressure and the energy thus spent in the resistance was wasted. In the new way the two motors are grouped in series first, so that the current must flow through one motor before it gets to the next (Fig. 68), and therefore but one-half the pressure can reach each motor. The energy passing through the first motor (which causes the reduction in pressure for the other) is not wasted, as it is doing useful work in turning the armature and increasing the turning moment necessary for starting the car.

Practically all new controllers in use today are made by the General Electric Co. and these controllers are divided into four classes, as follows:

Type B controllers, which may be either of the series parallel or rheostatic type but which always include the necessary contacts and connections for operating electric brakes.

Type K controllers is the series-parallel type, and is the type almost universally used. In these controllers one of the features is the shunting or short circuiting of one of the motors when changing from the series to the parallel connection.

Type L controllers are also of the series parallel type, but differ from type K controllers in that the circuit is completely opened when the change from series to parallel is made. Type R controllers are of the rheostatic type and are designed to control one or more motors by the use of resistance only.

One of the most important features of the General Electric controllers is the magnetic blow-out by means of which any arc forming between the controller terminals is blown out. Other important features are the cut-out switches and the interlocks. The cut-out switches are arranged so that either motor on the two-motor equipments, or either pair of motors on the four-motor equipments, may be cut out without impairing the operation of the remaining motors. The interlocks prevent, as far as possible, the abuse of the controller, as they make movement of any of the handles impossible unless the remaining handles are in such a position that no trouble can result. These controllers are built with hinge clamps, permitting the cover to swing open from either side, or to be completely removed. The parts of all these controllers are interchangeable, permitting ease of repair and renewal.

The series parallel controllers manufactured at the present time are as follows: K-2, capacity two 40-h.p. motors, 5 series and 4 parallel points; K-4, capacity four 30-h.p. motors, 5 series and 4 parallel points; K-6, two-80-h.p. or four-40-h.p. motors, 6 series and 5 parallel points; K-10, two 40-h.p. motors, 5 series, 4 parallel points; K-11, two 60-h.p. motors, 5 series and 4 parallel points; K-12, four 30-h.p. motors, 5 series and 4 parallel points; K-13, two 125-h.p. motors, 6 series, 6 parallel points; K-14, four 60-h.p. motors, 7 series, 6 parallel points; K-27, two 60-h.p. motors, 4 series, 4 parallel points; K-29, four 40-h.p. motors, 6 series and 5 parallel points; K-31, four 30-h.p. motors, 4 series and 4 parallel points; K-32, two 40-h.p. motors, 4 series and 4 parallel points; L-2, two 175-h.p. motors, 4 series and 4 parallel points; L-3, four 150-h.p. motors, 8 series and 7 parallel points; L-4, four 100-h.p. motors, 4 series, 4 parallel points; L-7, four 200-h.p. motors, 9 series, and 6 parallel points.

The electrical brake controllers are designated by the letter B and are as follows:

B-3, capacity two 40-h.p. motors, 4 series, 5 parallel and 6 brake points; B-7, two 100-h.p. motors, 6 series, 5 parallel and 6 brake points; B-8, four 60-h.p. motors, 6 series, 5 parallel and 7 brake points; B-13, two 40-h.p. motors, 5 series, 4 parallel and 7 brake points; B-18, two 40-h.p. motors, 4 series, 4 parallel and 6 brake points; B-19, four 40-h.p. motors, 5 series, 4 parallel, 7 brake points; B-23, two 60-h.p. motors, 5 series, 4 parallel and 7 brake points; B-29, two 60-h.p. motors, 5 series, 4 parallel and 7 brake points. The latter is similar to B-23, but has a separate brake handle.

The rheostatic controllers are designated by the letter R, and are made in the following capacities:

R-11 controller, capacity one 50-h.p. motor, 6 controlling points; R-14, two 35-h.p. motors, 5 points; R-15, two 80-h.p. motors, 6 points; R-16, four 40-h.p. motors, 5 points; R-17, one 50-h.p. motor, 6 points; R-19, two 50-h.p. motors, 6 points; R-22, two 50-h.p. motors, 5 points; R-29, four 125-h.p. motors, 6 points; R-37, two 50-h.p. motors, 5 points; R-38, two 35-h.p. motors, 5 points; R-48, four 75-h.p. motors, 8 points; R-55, two 150-h.p. motors, 7 points.

In the following descriptions of controllers there is included a number of controllers which are no longer manufactured, but many of these older controllers are still to be found on different roads where the old equipments have not yet been discarded, and it was therefore deemed advisable to include descriptions of the old as well as the modern controllers.

In Fig 74 is shown the type K-2 controller of the General Electric Company. On the top of the controller are visible two handles. The one located near the center of the controller top, called the controller handle, is attached to a spindle which passes through the whole length of the

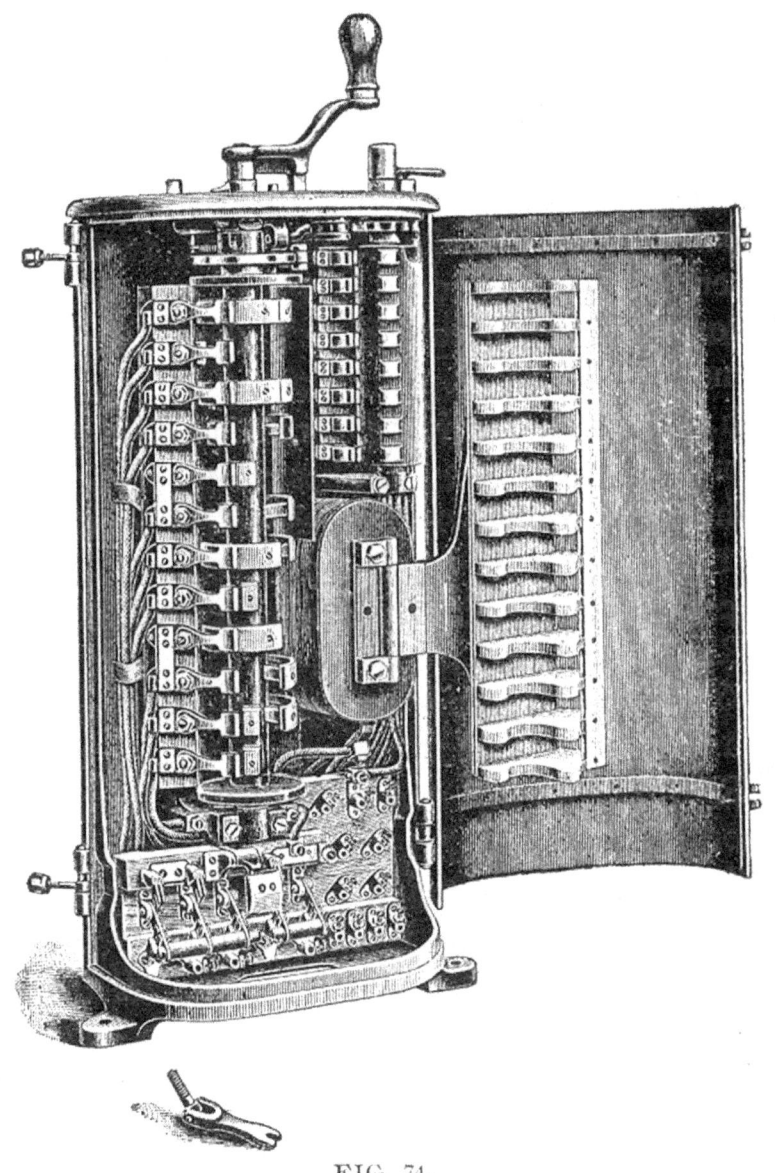

FIG. 74.

controller. On this spindle is mounted a cylinder by means of which the current is turned on to the motors. The second handle, called the reversing handle, is located at the right hand side and its purpose is to control the direction of the car. If this handle is pushed forward as far as it will go the car will go ahead when the controller handle is turned to close the circuit. The car will run backward when the reversing handle has been pulled to the other extreme position and the controller handle is operated as before. What takes place is this: The reversing lever operates a small drum inside of the controller which is provided with contacts. This handle has three positions. The working of this handle forward or backward changes the connections of the motor armatures so that the current flows through them in one direction when the car is to go ahead, and in the opposite direction when the car is to go backward, as explained in the previous chapter. When the reverse handle stands at the intermediate position between forward and reverse, the current is shut off from the motor at that controller and the reversing handle can be removed only when it is at this intermediate position. An interlocking arrangement prevents any movement of the reversing handle except when the large or power cylinder is at the "off" position. This same locking device prevents any movement of the power cylinder except when the reversing handle is fully thrown into proper position and standing at either "forward" or "backward."

The reversing cylinder, therefore, controls the direction in which the car moves. The propelling of the car and its speed is controlled by the controller handle with which the motorman has far more to do than with the one just described. We will, therefore, go fully into the details of changes that take place when the controller handle is shifted from one point to another.

On the top of the controller will be seen a number of points or dashes and on the spindle is fastened a finger or index which points to these raised marks as the handle is

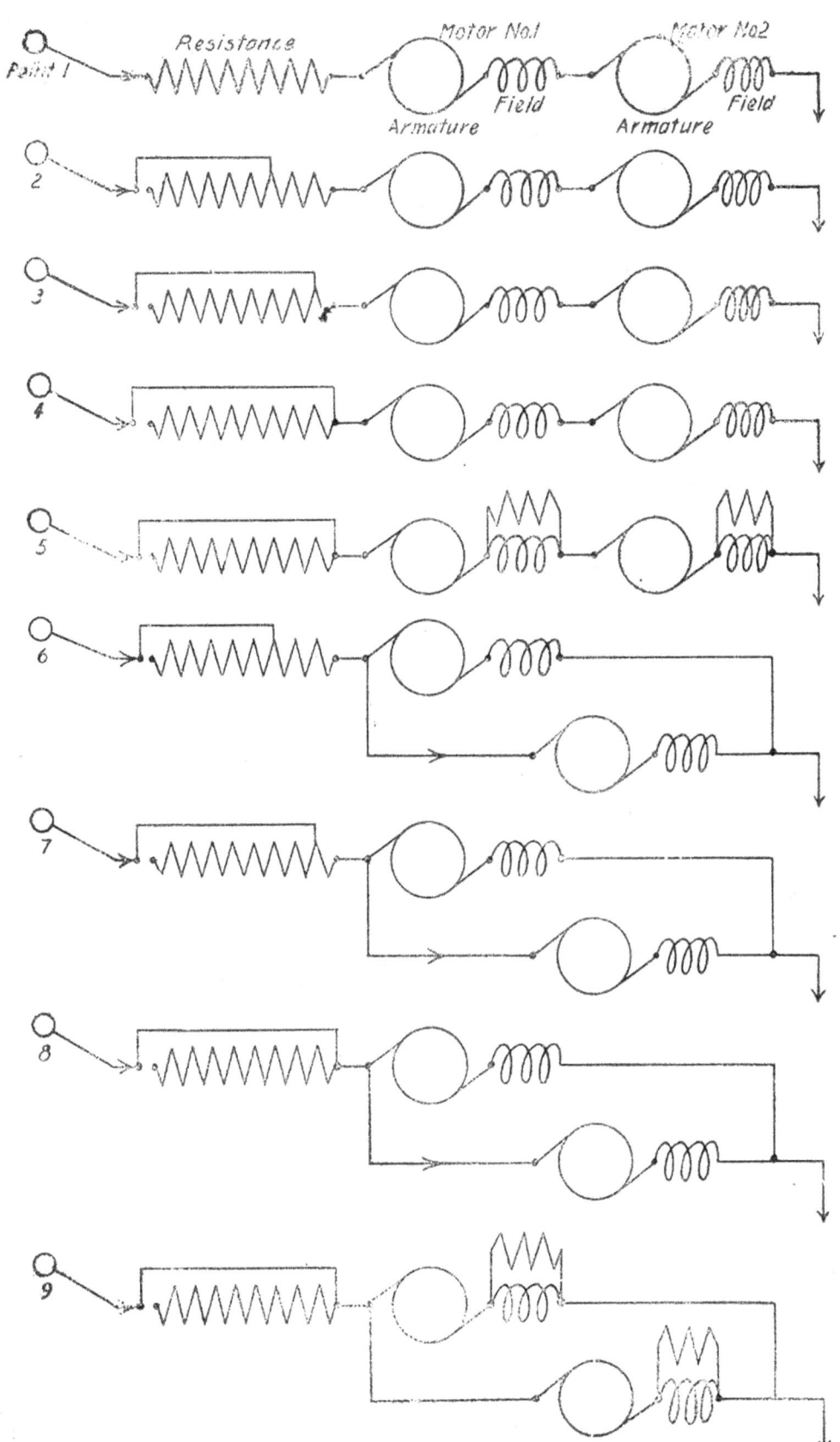

FIG. 75.

moved around to admit current to the motors. When the car is standing ready to start, the finger points to the position marked "off." To start the car, the handle is moved around in the direction of the hands of a watch to the first point. This connects the motors and resistance to the circuit so that the current flows first through the iron plates of the resistance, then through one of the motors, then through the other motor, and finally to the ground through the car truck, wheels and rails. The motors are in this case what is technically known as connected in "series." This is represented in the diagram showing the connections on the first point in Fig. 75. The connections made on all the following points of this controller are also shown in the same figure and should be studied while reading this explanation. On the second point, the connections, it will be seen, remain the same as on the first, except that two-thirds of the resistance has been cut out of the circuit, so that more current may reach the motors. On the third point, eleven-twelfths of the resistance is cut out of the circuit and on the fourth point, all the resistance is out so that the current flows only through the two motors in series.

All resistance is now cut out and no power is being wasted as the current is doing only useful work in the motors. We can therefore keep the controller on this point for any length of time with economy, only the car will run a little less than half its maximum speed. To increase the speed still more, we move the controller to the fifth point. In doing this, connections are made so that part of the current is shunted through a resistance around the field coils of the motor; that is, instead of having all the current that flows through the armatures flow also through the fields, a part of it is made to take a by-pass or shunt around the fields. This has the effect of increasing the speed of the motors and they will on this point run at half the full speed.

In moving the controller to the sixth point, an important change is made in the connections of the motors.

As said before, when the controller is on the fourth and fifth points, the motors are in series with each other, the current flowing first through one and then through the other. Consequently each motor gets only one-half the pressure of voltage between the trolley wire and ground. That is to say, by the time that the current has passed through the first motor, half of the pressure has been used, leaving only the remaining half to run the other motor. To increase the speed we must now connect the motors so that they both will get the full pressure from the trolley line. This cannot be done abruptly, however, but some resistance must be introduced into the circuit at the time this change is made to prevent the car from jerking, just as it would have acted on the first point had some resistance not been interposed when first starting. Therefore, on the sixth point, the motors are connected so that the current divides and half flows through each motor. They are then what is technically called connected in "parallel." They both get the full pressure, except that some resistance is put in the circuit before the current gets to the motors. A part of this resistance is cut out on the seventh point. On the eighth point all of the resistance is out and the motors are connected so that they both get the full pressure and run at nearly full speed. On the ninth point part of the current is shunted around the field coils as on the fifth point, and the motors run at their highest speed. At each point there is provided a notch on a wheel or ratchet, mounted on the controller spindle inside the controller case, which prevents the handle from stopping between points when it is turned.

At the lower end of the controller are located the motor cut-out switches, which enables one to operate a car with a single motor should the other one have become defective.

When it is desired to have both motors in operation, as is generally the case, both switches should be down. The operator will find an instruction card in each controller reading either—

> **To CUT OUT MOTOR No. 1** (motor nearest—**THIS**—end of car) throw up left hand switch as far as it will go.
> **To CUT OUT MOTOR No. 2** (motor nearest—**THE OTHER**—end of car) throw up right hand switch as far as it will go.

> **To CUT OUT MOTOR No. 1** (motor nearest—**THE OTHER**—end of car) throw up left hand switch as far as it will go.
> **To CUT OUT MOTOR No. 2** (motor nearest—**THIS**—end of car) throw up right hand switch as far as it will go.

It will be noticed that they do not read alike on the two controllers of the same car. This is due to the difference in connection. Should at any time it become necessary to cut out a motor, look for the instruction card in the controller stand. To operate with a single motor, the car will start on point 1 and reach its full speed on point 5. A stop is placed on the controller spindle, with which a pin engages, preventing movement of the controller cylinder beyond the fifth point. This is effected by either of these cut-out switches, which, in being raised, operate the pin.

The high controlling lever on the top (Fig. 74) turns the central shaft, on which are mounted the contact pieces or sections, which, when the shaft is turned, will establish connections with the stationary terminals located to the left.

The wires to the left connect with the terminal board in the controller to which are also attached the wires going to the motors and to the second controller and resistance boxes.

The old K controller of the General Electric Co. is very similar to the K-2. It was of earlier construction than the K-2, but as the K-2 has been most widely used, it was considered best to give it the more detailed description. The K controller is about 2 in. shorter than the K-2 and its appearance is almost the same. It has, however, two points less; in other respects its mechanical contruction is the same.

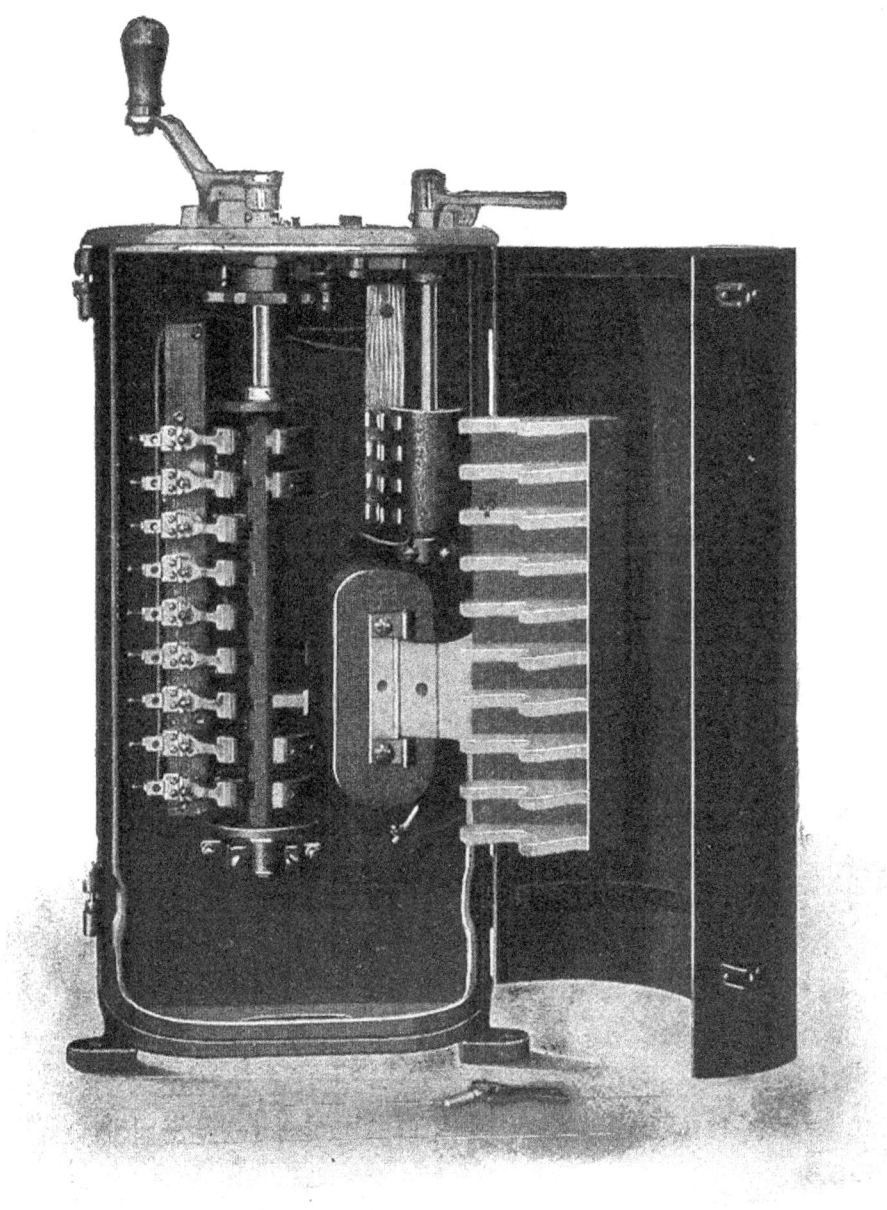

FIG. 76.

The old style or rheostat controllers of this company, known as types 51 and 83, and described in the first part of this chapter, have been gradually superseded by the R type of controllers previously mentioned. A controller of this type R-17, is shown in Fig. 76.

The K-4 controller is used in connection with larger cars,

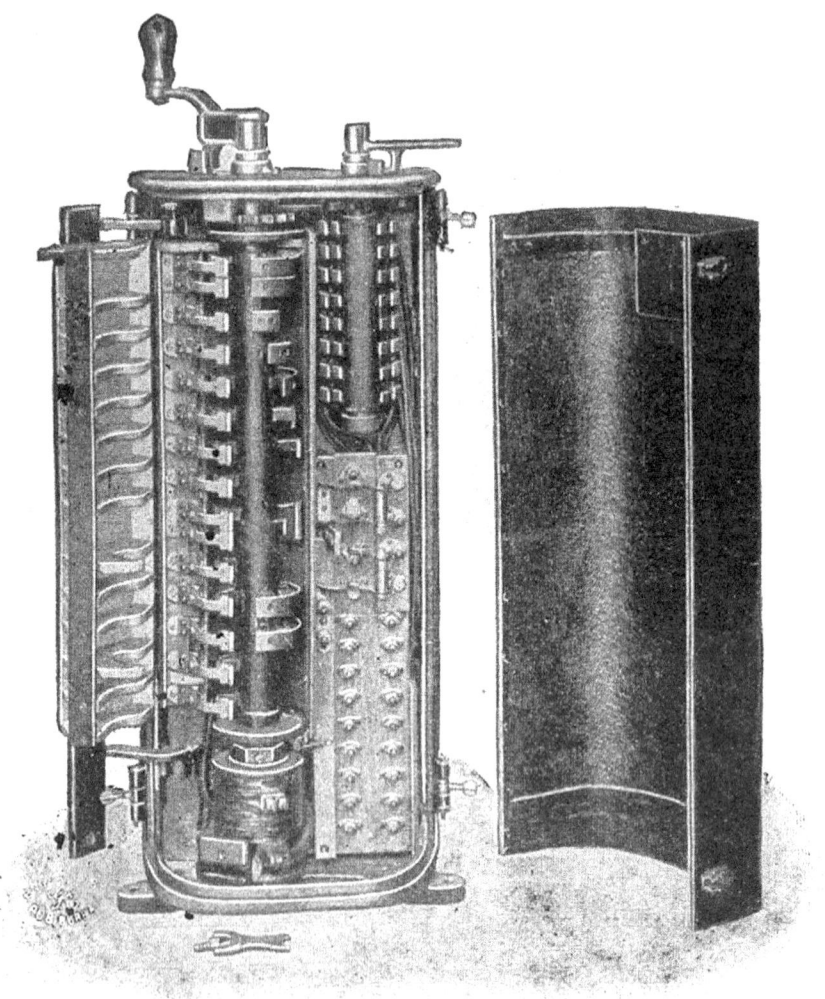

FIG. 77.

where four motors instead of two are mounted on the trucks. Its action is like the K-2 controller, and the difference is that instead of having first two motors in series and later in parallel, as there are in this case, two identical sets of motors of two motors per set. Each set of two motors is permanently grouped in parallel, and the one pair is first placed in series with the other pair or set, and finally the two series are connected in parallel.

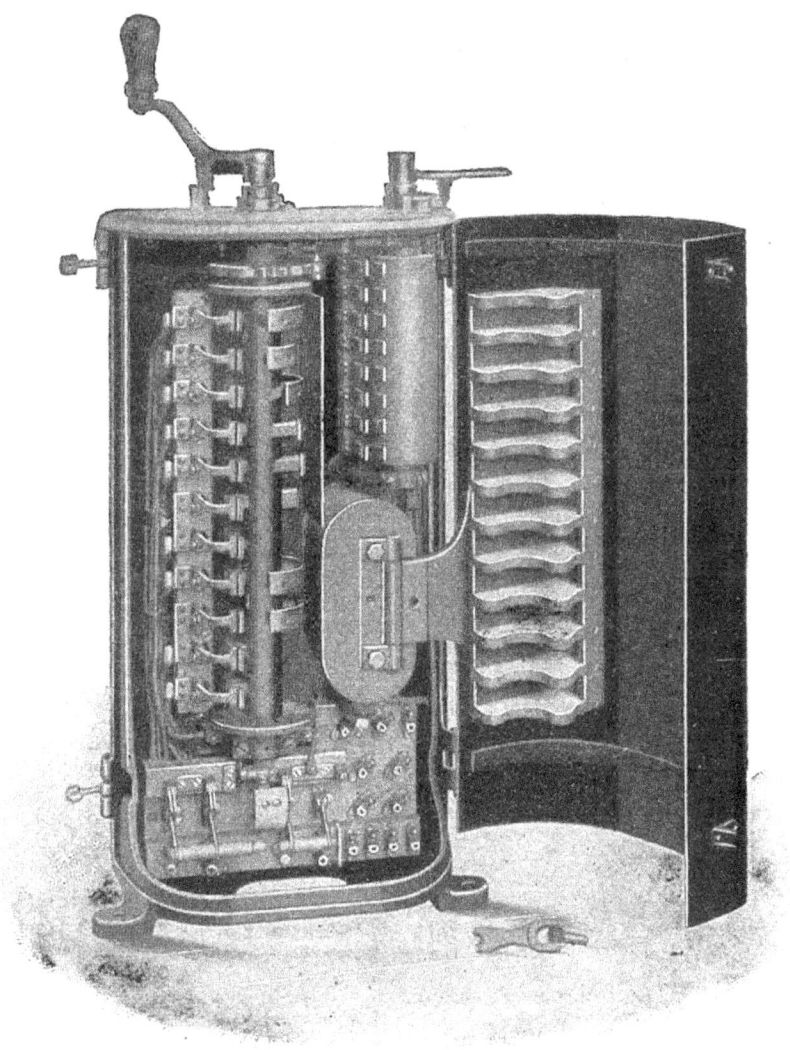

FIG. 78.

The old K-21 controller is the same as the K-2, except that it is of greater capacity, as its contacts and wires are larger.

The K-6 controller which is designed for two 80-h.p. motors or four 40-h. p. motors is shown in Fig. 77.

The K-10 controller is designed for two 40-h. p. motors. It is a controller with nine notches. On the first four notches the motors are in series and resistance in circuit. On the fifth notch motors are in series with resistance all cut out. On the sixth, seventh and eighth, motors are in parallel and resistance in circuit. The ninth is for full speed, motors in multiple. The K-10 controller is shown in Fig. 78. Field shunts are not used with this controller.

The K-11 controller is the same as the K-10, except it is designed for heavier currents and larger motors.

The K-12 controller is like the K-11, except that it is made to operate four motors in two sets just as the K-4.

The K-13 is designed for two 125-h. p. motors. It is a thirteen notch controller. The motors are in series up to and on the seventh point. From the eighth to the thirteenth they are in multiple. The preferred running notches are the seventh and thirteenth. No field shunts are used.

The K-14 is for four 60-h. p. motors and is like the K-13, except that it handles four motors in two groups as the K-4.

The old K-15 controller is practically a double K-13, with two controlling drums and two 125-h. p. motors controlled by each drum. The notches are the same as on the K-13.

The old K-16 controller is the same as K-15, but with different case.

The K-27 controller is similar to the K-11, but is arranged for operation on a metallic circuit, having contacts for opening both sides of the circuit.

The K-29 controller is similar to the K-6, but has contacts for opening both sides of the circuit.

The K-31 controller is similar to the K-27, but has reverse switch arranged for four motors.

The K-32 controller is also similar to the K-27, but is of smaller capacity.

The L-2 controller is used for two 175-h. p motors, and

the L-4 for four 100-h. p. motors. They have four points in series and four in multiple. The handle is operated contrary to the hands of a watch, or in the opposite direction

FIG. 79.

from most controllers. The first half revolution moves the controller through the series points and brings them into full series. To throw them into multiple the movement of the handle of the controller is continued on around to the original off position, and when the handle begins to pass over what were the series notches on the first revolution, the motors are thrown in multiple, so that when the handle has completed a revolution and a half the motors are connected for full speed in multiple. The current is always off when the handle is at the left and always on when it is at the right. A brass dial on top of the controller indicates whether the motors are in series or multiple.

The L-3 controller for four 150-h. p. motors has 15 points, eight series and seven parallel. This controller is shown in Fig. 79.

The L-7 controller for four 200-h. p. motors has 15 points, nine series and six parallel.

The General Electric Company's controllers for use with electric brakes are known as the B type. The action of the electric brake and the way to operate it is described later on in the chapter on brakes. Some of these controllers have a double set of points or notches. Moving the handle in the usual way from off position starts the car just as on other controllers. Moving the handle the other way from off position applies the electric brake, if the car is running. The capacities of the B controllers at present manufactured and the number of controlling points on each has been already shown in this chapter. The B-8 controller has separate handles for power and brake as is also the case with the B-7, B-19 and the B-29.

The B-23 controller is shown in Fig. 80, and has but one power and brake handle. The B-3, B-13 and B-18 also have only one handle which is operated in one direction for the power and in the other direction for the brake, as just described. Of the B controllers the B-13 is most generally used and its braking connections are such as to render the skidding of the wheels practically impossible.

The Westinghouse Electric & Manufacturing Co. formerly manufactured controllers of which a number was of the series-parallel type. The Westinghouse controllers are no longer made, but as many of them will be found in use on

FIG. 80.

different roads, a description of them is given. The old Westinghouse series-parallel controllers and their coresponding diverters are known as—

Controllers	Diverters
G.	E.
No. 14	No. 7
No. 28	No. 46
No. 28A	No. 46 or 47
No. 29	No. 47
No. 38	No. 38

With the rapid advancement and development of electric street railroads more powerful motors were required, and at the same time greater economy in consumption of power was the object aimed at by the manufacturers. Owing to these developments and advancements the parallel controller D, described at the beginning of the chapter, has not been manufactured for several years.

In the center of the G controller cover plate is located the controller handle for regulating the speed of the car. On the right-hand side, through the rim of the cover plate, extends a straight handle or lever, which is the reversing handle. The two raised lugs to the left on the cover are stops which prevent the controller lever from going round to make a complete circle. At the front lug the handle is at the "off" position. The cylinder contacts are disconnected from the contact fingers in this position and the car is at rest. When the handle is turned so far as to strike the other lug the highet speed is reached. The reverse handle, which should be moved only when the controller handle is in the "off" position, has three notches. The central position opens the circuit and cuts off the current; the outward and the inward position control the direction in which the car travels, either forward or back. If the handle is pushed forward as far as possible, the car will go ahead when the current is turned on by the controller handle. Pulling the handle inward (toward one's self or toward the car) reverses the armature connections, so that the car backs or run backward when the controller handle is moved from the "off" position to the first notch. The contacts controlled by this reversing handle are mounted on a small vulcabeston disk which is secured in the inside of the controller cover. All the terminals and contact fingers, as well as the rings on the drum, are separated from one another by vulcabeston partitions which project between them and the rings. Their object is to prevent the current from jumping from one terminal to the next.

The first G controllers had ratchet wheels with 10 notches. Only the first three notches or controller positions and the last three are "running" positions (namely, the positions in which the controller handle may remain for some time to operate the car), while the other four should be passed over slowly, but without stopping on any one of them for more than a moment.

In the later G controllers, the ratchet wheels had only the six running notches, the intermediate four being omitted. The changes that take place on the various positions are enumerated below and may be readily followed by the diagram shown in Fig. 81. The reversing handle being in the forward position, the car will go ahead when the controller handle is operated. Moving the controller handle from the "off" position to the first notch will close the circuit and connect the controllers, motors and diverter resistance to the trolley line and to the ground return or rail. Both motors are then in series connections with one another and also in series with the whole diverter resistance. This is the starting position; the mtors receive each less than half the pressure of the line. This slow speed can be used especially in crowded streets. Moving the controller handle to the second notch has the effect of short circuiting or cutting out of active service one-half of the diverter resistance. This allows a heavier current to flow through the motors, resulting in increased speed.

Moving controller handle to the third notch causes the controller drum to cut out all the resistance, and now the

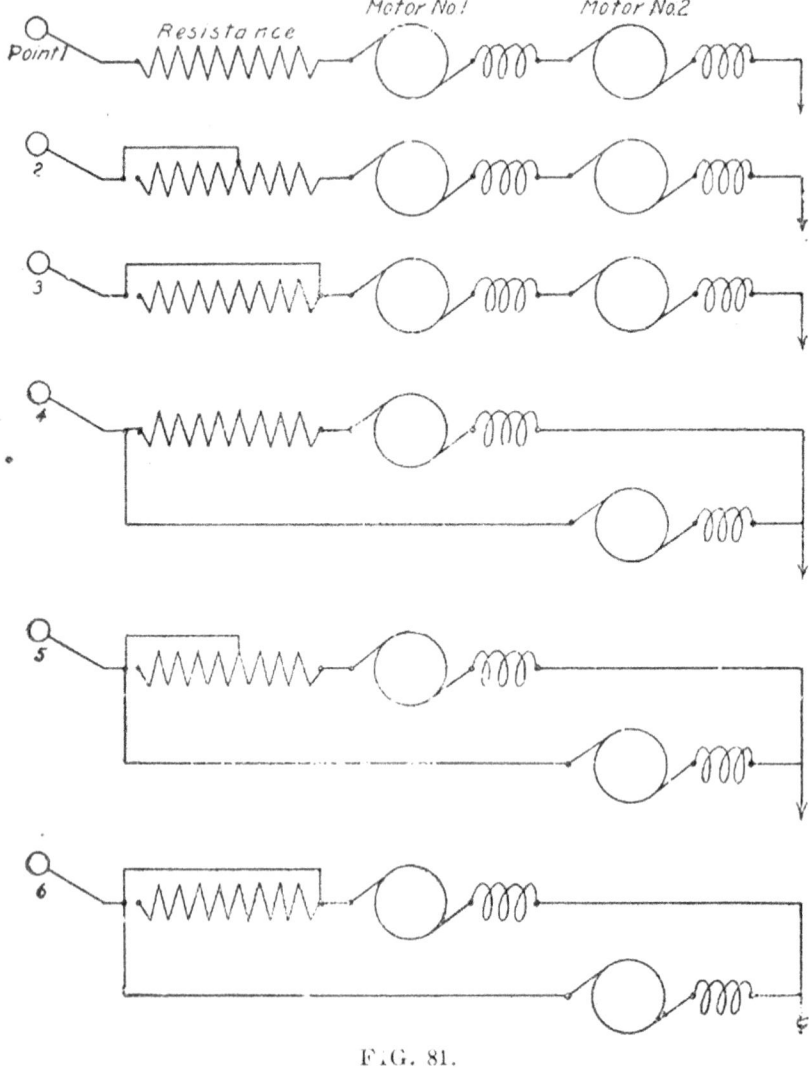

FIG. 81.

two motors are in series with one another and receive the total voltage of the line. Each one is working under half the total pressure. The position is an economical one and the speed is half full speed. The controller may remain in this position for any length of time. Between the third and fourth notches several intermediate connections are made between the diverter and motors. However, as these are made in succession and without stopping, and are not operating positions, they are omitted from the ratchet, and when the handle arrives at the fourth notch both motors have changed from the series to the parallel connection, and the diverter resistance is in series circuit with one of them. This is the next higher speed. In the fifth notch half of the diverter resistance is cut out, but the relations of the motors is unchanged. The speed is further increased. Neither the fourth nor the fifth notch should be used for any great length of time. In the sixth position, at which the motors reach their highest speed, all resistance is cut out of the circuit and both motors are in parallel, each receiving the full pressure of the line.

The No. 14 Westinghouse controller is in outward appearance very similar to the G controller. It has, however, a number of modifications which should be noted. The controller drum is mounted so to swing outward, for the purpose of easily examining or to have access to all parts, as in the G controller. Further, there is provided an interlocking device between the controller and the reversing device. To remove either it is necessary to bring the handle to the "off" position, namely, into that position in which the current is cut off from the trolley. Lastly, this controller is provided further with motor cut-out switches or plugs. It was at first the custom of the Westinghouse company to place the motor cut-outs under the seats in the car. This method was later abandoned, and plugs were provided inside of the controller casting on the right-hand side. The various changes made with this controller will be given in a short and concise way. The changes are more gradual and the work is more evenly distributed than with the G controller. In principle it is very similar to the operation of the G controller, and therefore it is believed that with this controller, and all the following that are described of the Westinghouse make, the simple enumeration of the change will suffice. In this controller the reversing switch changes the connections of the motor field coils to cause the armature to rotate in the opposite direction.

Moving the controller handle from the "off" position to notch 1, both motors are connected in series with one another and in series with all the diverter resistance between trolley and rail. This is the starting position and slowest speed.

On notch 2 both motors are in series with each other and the diverter resistance, with some of the resistance short circuited, causing an increased current to pass the motors and resulting in higher speed.

Notch 3. The whole resistance is cut out of action and the two motors, still in series with one another, are receiving the total line pressure, that is, each one receives half of this pressure. The cutting out of all the resistance further increases the motor speed.

Notch 4. Between notch 3 and 4 there are a number of intermediate combinations which follow in rapid succession, and when contact is established in notch 4 the motors are no longer in series. Each motor is in series with half of the resistance, and one motor and resistance are grouped in parallel with the other one and resistance, resulting in increase of speed over notch 3.

Notch 5. The resistance is cut out of circuit of one of the motors which receives the total line pressure. It remains in parallel with the other motor which has still half of the resistance in series with it. Speed in this notch is higher than on notch 4.

Notch 6. The resistance is also cut out of the circuit of the second motor, therefore no resistance is in the circuit.

The motors are in parallel, each receiving the full line pressure, resulting in maximum speed.

If at any time it becomes necessary to cut out one of the motors, the upper plug will cut out motor number 1, the lower plug motor number 2. Running with the one motor only the car will not start when controller is moved to notch 1, but it has to be placed on notch 4, which is the starting position under these conditions.

The Nos. 28 and 29 Westinghouse controllers are both similar in construction and operation to the No. 14. The difference is mainly of a mechanical nature. The No. 28 is of smaller dimensions than the No. 14, while the No. 29 is built heavier, to control more powerful motors and currents. The grouping of the circuits by these controllers is very similar to that of the No. 14. The main difference is that the resistance is not divided between the two motors, and any change made in it affects both motors exactly the same way.

Notch 1. Motor No. 1, motor No. 2 and diverter all in series.

Notch 2. Motor No. 1, motor No. 2 and part of resistance in series.

Notch 3. Motor No. 1, motor No. 2, in series, resistance all out of action.

Notch 4. Motor No. 1, motor No. 2, in parellel, resistance in series with both of them.

Notch 5. Motor No. 1, motor No. 2, in parallel, part of diverter cut-out, rest in series with both motors.

Notch 6. Motor No. 1, motor No. 2, in parallel between the line receiving full pressure, all resistance being cut out. Highest speed obtainable.

When but one motor is used the car will not start before the fourth notch is reached.

The 28A Westinghouse controller is heavier in all its

parts and had many changes of a mechanical nature. To begin with, the reversing handle as well as the controller handle was placed on top of the controller cover. They were made to interlock to prevent the moving of the reversing handle when the controller handle is not in the "off" position. This controller has seven notches or running positios, and in case that one of the motors is cut out, the car will start with the first notch and reach maximum speed in the fourth position, beyond which the handle will not turn. A latch is provided which automatically locks the drum when either one of the motor cut-out plugs at the lower right-hand side of the controller is removed. The controller changes are as follows:

Notch 1. Motor 1, motor 2 and total resistance in series with one another.

Notch 2. Motor 1, and motor 2, in series with less resistance.

Notch 3. Same as 2, with still less resistance.

Notch 4. Motors 1 and 2, in series without resistance.

Notch 5. Motors 1 and 2, in parallel with part of resistance in series.

Notch 6. Motors 1 and 2, in parallel with less resistance.

Notch 7. Motors 1 and 2, in parallel without any resistance.

The Westinghouse No. 38 controller was designed for large cars and motors. Its general arrangement is like No. 28A as to interlocking of controller and reversing handles as well as motor cut-out switches, and it was the largest controller for this service. Only the controllers used for locomotives are larger and heavier as regards the internal parts. It has four more contact rings than the 14, 28, 28A and 29. There are eight notches or positions for the controller handle.

Notch 1. Motors in series with one another and full resistance.

Notch 2. Conditions as before, but with less resistance.

Notch 3. Motors as before, with still less resistance in series.

Notch 4. The two motors in series, resistance entirely cut out.

Notch 5. Motors in parallel, with a part of the diverter resistance in series with both motors.

Notch 6. Motors as on 5, some resistance cut out.

Notch 7. Motors as on 6 and some more resistance cut out.

Notch 8. Motors in parallel as on 7 and all resistance cut out. Maximum speed.

When one of the motors is cut out of circuit and the car is operated by the other, it will start when controller handle is moved into the first notch and reaches maximum speed in the fourth.

The diverter box is the same as a resistance box. It is made of iron bands wound into flat iron coils of spiral shape, separated by mica. They must be of different sizes depending on the capacity of the motors. The heavier the current that is supplied to a motor, the wider has to be the iron spiral, to prevent overheating.

The Walker Company's Controllers.—The Walker Company had a number of controllers on the market, but few, if any, of these will be found in use at present. One is the J type. The reversing handle is at the right. In this controller there are no separate switches or plugs provided for cutting out any one motor, these provisions being made on the reversing cylinder, so that this one handle can accomplish all these functions, as will be described later on. The controller has five running notches, and the resistance is of such capacity that any one of these notches may be used for continuous service, though not with economy. Another point in construction to be mentioned is that the controller is provided with a magnetic lock, which renders it impossible to move the reverse handle when current is flowing through the controller. The construction is such that when the circuit is opened contact is broken simul-

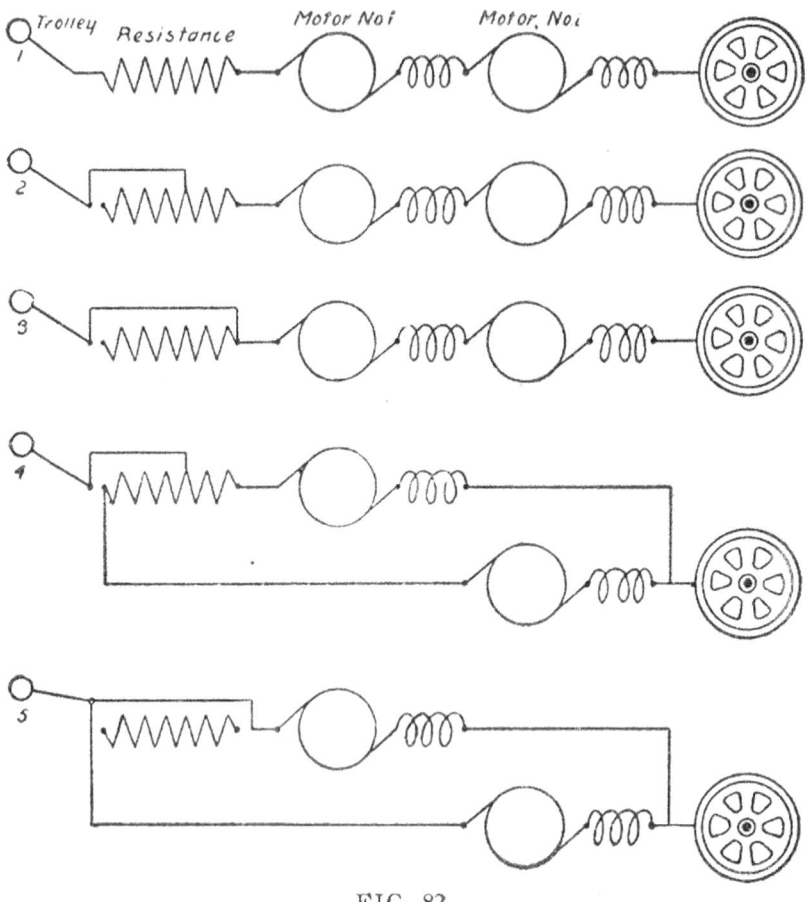

FIG. 82.

taneously at eight different places, thereby greatly overcoming the bad arc that otherwise would exist if it was broken at one or two places only. In this controller, as in all others, every terminal is lettered so as to prevent confusion. These letters are for the benefit of the electrician or wireman who wires the cars, sets up the motors and makes the connections.

The combinations with this controller are as follows (see Fig. 82):

First point. Motors in series; all the resistance in circuit.

Second point. Motors in series and the current only flowing through one-half the rheostat.

Third point. The two motors are in series with the rheostat entirely cut out.

Fourth point. The current now flows from the trolley to the center of the rheostat, and is equally divided between the two motors, which are in parallel.

Fifth point. Motors in parallel, resistance all out.

There are six positions of the reverse cylinder. In the normal "off" position the handle of the reverse cylinder stands parallel with the face of the controller, pointing to the right. In this position both motors are cut out. If now the handle is pushed forward until it comes in contact with the stop, both motors are connected so as to carry the car forward. If the handle is pulled backward until it comes in contact with the stop, both motors are connected in such a direction as to carry the car backwards. To cut out one motor, raise the reverse handle about ¾ in., far enough to clear the stop and turn the cylinder until the handle points to the left. If it is now pushed forward against the stop, so as to cover the point marked "1," No. 1 motor only is in action propelling the car forward, while No. 2 motor is cut out. Pull the reverse handle back about 45°, or an eighth of a turn, until it covers point marked "2," and No. 2 motor only is in action, carrying the car forward, while No. 1 motor is cut out. Pulling it still farther back until it comes in contact with the stop and covers point marked "1," we have again No. 1 motor in action, carrying the car backwards. Moving it forward from here about 45° until it covers the other point marked "2," we have again **No. 2** motor in action, carrying the car backwards.

These combinations give us, therefore, on the controller one forward point for both motors, one for No. 1 and one for No. 2, and the three reverse positions corresponding to these. In running on No. 1 motor alone, either forward or back, the car does not "take power" until the controller handle reaches the fourth point. With No. 1 motor the car "takes power" between the third and fourth points.

The last controller made by the Walker Company was the type S. In this car controller a solenoid or coil of wire

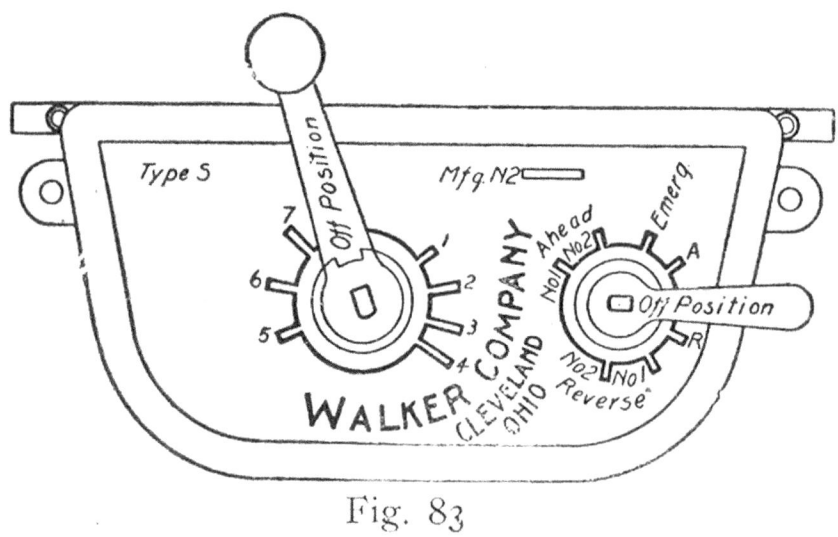

Fig. 83

is used between each contact ring. This is to prevent the burning of the contact rings and fingers by the electric arc which forms when a circuit is opened. The magnetism caused by the solenoid or coil blows out the arcs as soon as they form. Fig. 83 shows the plan of this controller top with the handles at "off" position. It will be seen that there are seven points on this controller. On the first four the motors are in series and on the last three in parallel.

The reverse lever on this controller differs from that on other controllers in several respects. Looking at the surface plate diagram, Fig. 83, we see the various reverse lever points indicated around the reverse lever at the right. The point marked No. 1 ahead means that when the reverse lever is put over to that point, motor No. 1 will run the car ahead, No. 2 being cut out, and so on for the other points. The position marked A means that on this both motors will act together to drive the car ahead, while R means that both motors will reverse. The other points will explain themselves, all but the one marked "Emerg.," which is an emergency electric brake for stopping the car quickly in emergencies in place of reversing it. All that is necessary to do to operate this brake is to shut off current with the controller handle and then put the reverse handle on the emergency brake position. After this is done begin to apply the hand brake. The emergency electric brake acts by turning the motors into dynamos by changing their connections and causing them to generate current to stop themselves.

Controller of the Steel Motor Company.—This company has built various controllers since 1892. The last and most improved type is known as the 43 controller. It was made very simple by reducing the number of terminals and connections. This controller differed from others in that wires from the car cables did not go to a terminal board, but instead directly to the contact fingers of the controller.

Arcing at the opening of the circuit it subdued by providing two coils placed on either side of the controlling cylinder or drum and partially enveloping it, the drum acting as the core of an electro magnet. The current passes through the coils before a connection is made with the motors.

The reverse and cut-out switches are combined. An index shows the positions to which the reverse handle is moved in order to run both motors together or either of them independently in either direction. The reverse handle cannot be removed except when the circuit is open. In ordinary practice the motors can be reversed without shutting off the current, but the cam index on the inside is so designed that the addition of a common iron washer provides the necessary device to prevent this. There are nine points of contact, and when used without a shunt across the fields,

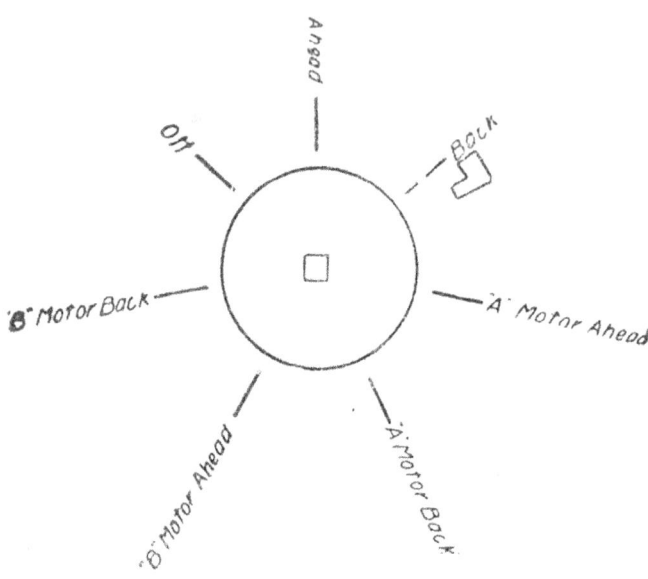

FIG. 84.

two of them are running positions; when used with a shunt, there are three running positions.

At "off" position the controller handle is at about the same place as on other series-parallel controllers, and to start the car it is moved clock-wise. The connections made are as follows:

First point. Motors are in series with all resistance in circuit.

Second point. Motors in series, about two-thirds of the resistance in circuit.

Third point. Motors in series, about one-third of resistance in circuit.

Fourth point. Motors in series with all resistance cut out. After passing fourth contact, circuit is broken and both motors are put in multiple.

Fifth point. Motors in multiple with full resistance in series circuit with them.

Sixth point. Motors in multiple with two-thirds of resistance in series with both motors.

Seventh point. Motors in multiple with one-third of resistance in series with them.

Eighth point. Motors in multiple, no resistance.

Ninth point. If motors are operated with a shunt this is brought into service on the ninth contact. If no shunt is used the ninth point does not produce any change over point 8, and operates the motors in precisely the same manner as the eighth.

The effect produced by each notch of the reverse and cut-out switch is indicated by the copy of the index around the reverse switch shown in Fig. 84.

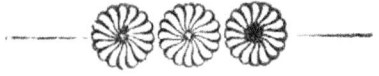

CHAPTER IV.

MULTIPLE UNIT SYSTEMS.

In the previous chapter was explained the method of controlling motor cars when run singly or when towing one or more trail cars not equipped with motors. On some electric railways where the traffic is heavy it becomes necessary to run trains of several cars, some or all of which are motor cars. It also becomes necessary at times to divide these trains into smaller ones or to add more cars as the traffic fluctuates, and as it is obviously unpractical to have more than one motorman to drive a train means must be provided so that each motor car of the train may be controlled from the front of the train by one man. This method of control is generally known as the multiple unit system of control. One of these multiple controllers is placed at each end of each motor car and they are so arranged that when the controller at the front end of the train is moved to any particular notch, all the other controllers on the train are automatically moved to the same position, so that while the train is operated as a whole from one controller each car is operated independently by its own controller. The multiple unit system allows the greatest flexibility in the operation of cars, for one car can be run alone or any number of cars may be coupled together, each car being driven by its own motor as an independent unit.

Owing to the large amount of current required to operate electric cars the multiple unit system is generally operated on the third rail system described in Chapter VI. The contact area of the ordinary trolley wheel with the trolley wire is too small to carry the current required for a heavy train of cars and as the use of several trolleys on one train would be too troublesome, the current is taken from a third rail alongside the track, by means of sliding contacts or shoes carried on each car. There are two systems of multiple control in use, that of the General Electric Co., known as the type M control, which is electrically operated, and the Westinghouse multiple control system which is operated by means of compressed air.

In the type M control the series parallel motor controller as described in the previous chapter is replaced by a number of electrically operated switches, called contactors, which are placed under each motor car, and there is also a separate electrically operated reversing switch called the reverser. These contactors and the reverser fulfill the same functions as the controllers on a single car, making the same combination of the motors and starting resistances. Instead, however, of being directly operated by the motorman they are operated through a small controller, called the master controller, to which all the conductors and reversers on the train are attached by means of a control circuit cable. This cable runs the entire length of the train and is connected from car to car by means of suitable couplers, and when trail cars are placed between motor cars they are also provided with cables. The platforms of each motor car and, if desired, those of each trail car are equipped with a master controller so that the train may be operated from the platform of whichever car happens to be in front.

The master controller, type C 6, shown in Fig. 85, although smaller than the ordinary car controller, is similar in appearance, and method of operation. It has separate power and reverse handles and it contains a magnetic blow-out similar to that of the ordinary controller. All the current for the operation of the conductors is taken from the line and passes directly through whichever master controller hap-

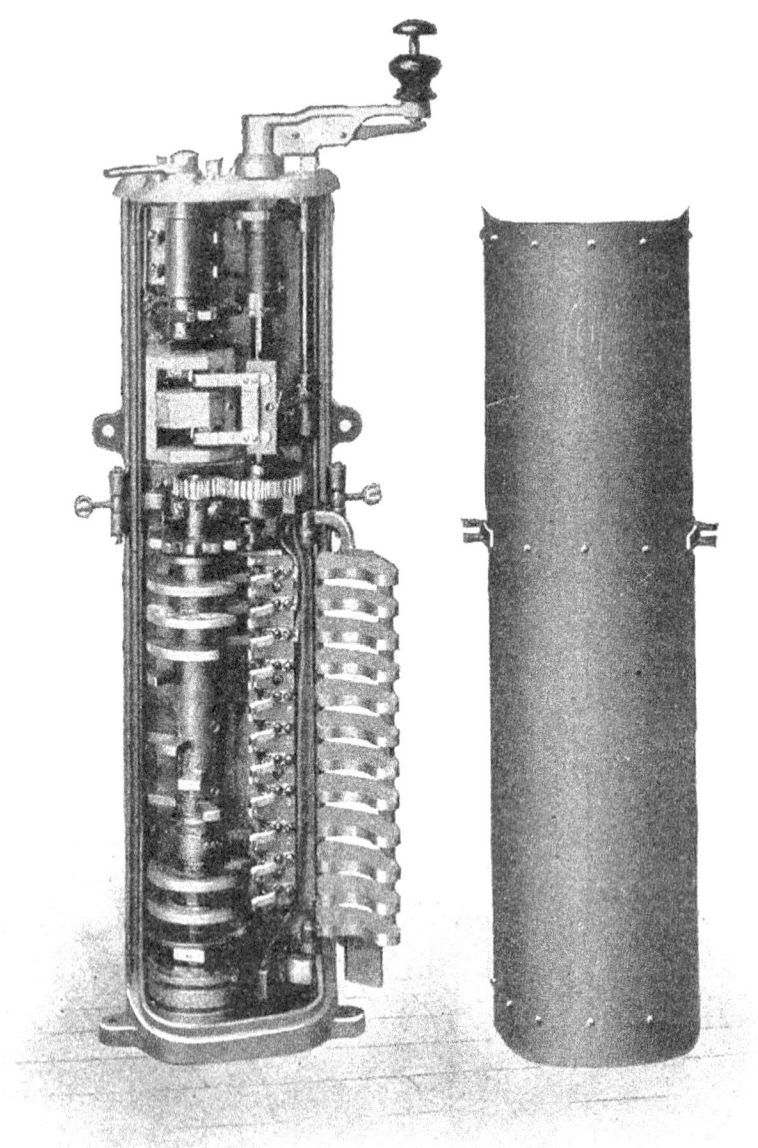

FIG. 85.

pens to be in use, and the handle of the master controller is generally arranged so that if the motorman removes his hand from it the control circuit will be broken and the contactors opened, thus shutting off all current from the motors. The reverse handle can only be removed when it is in the off position and the power handle is mechanically locked when the reverse handle is removed.

The contactors each consist of a movable arm with a removable copper contact at one end, making contact with a similar fixed contact piece, and a coil which actuates the arm when supplied with current from the master controller. The contactor is closed only when the current of the control circuit passes through its coil and gravity, assisted by the spring action of the contact piece, causes the arm to drop and the circuit to open when the control circuit is broken. The contactor also has a powerful magnetic blow-out. The reverser is somewhat similar to the ordinary reversing switch with the addition of electro-magnets for turning it either to the forward or reverse positions. Its operating coils are similar to those of the contactors. A cut-out switch is also provided by means of which all of the control operating circuits on any car may be cut out.

It will be evident from the foregoing explanation that there are two principal circuits on a car equipped with the type M control: First, the control circuit which passes from the line to the contact shoe on the car, thence to the master controller, thence through the various operating coils of the contactors and reversers and thence to the ground return; Second, the motor circuit, which from the contact shoe passes through the various contactors, thence to the motor fields and armatures and thence to the ground return. All of the contactors under each car taken together constitute a series parallel controller and the different combinations of the contactors is indicated by the position of the master controller handle. The diagram, Fig. 86, shows the complete connections of the C-6 controller and its auxiliary apparatus for a two-motor equipment. The running points on this con-

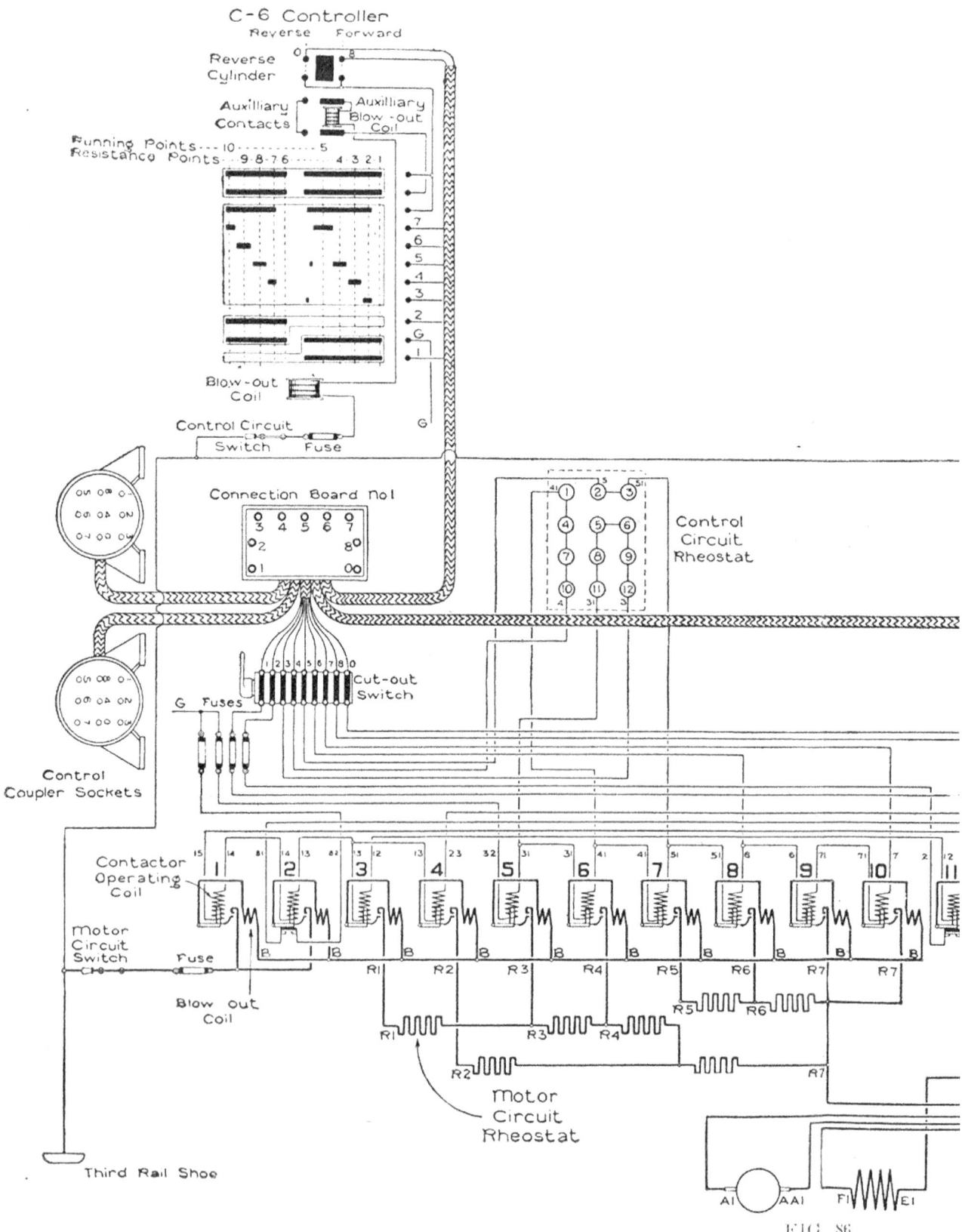

FIG. 86.

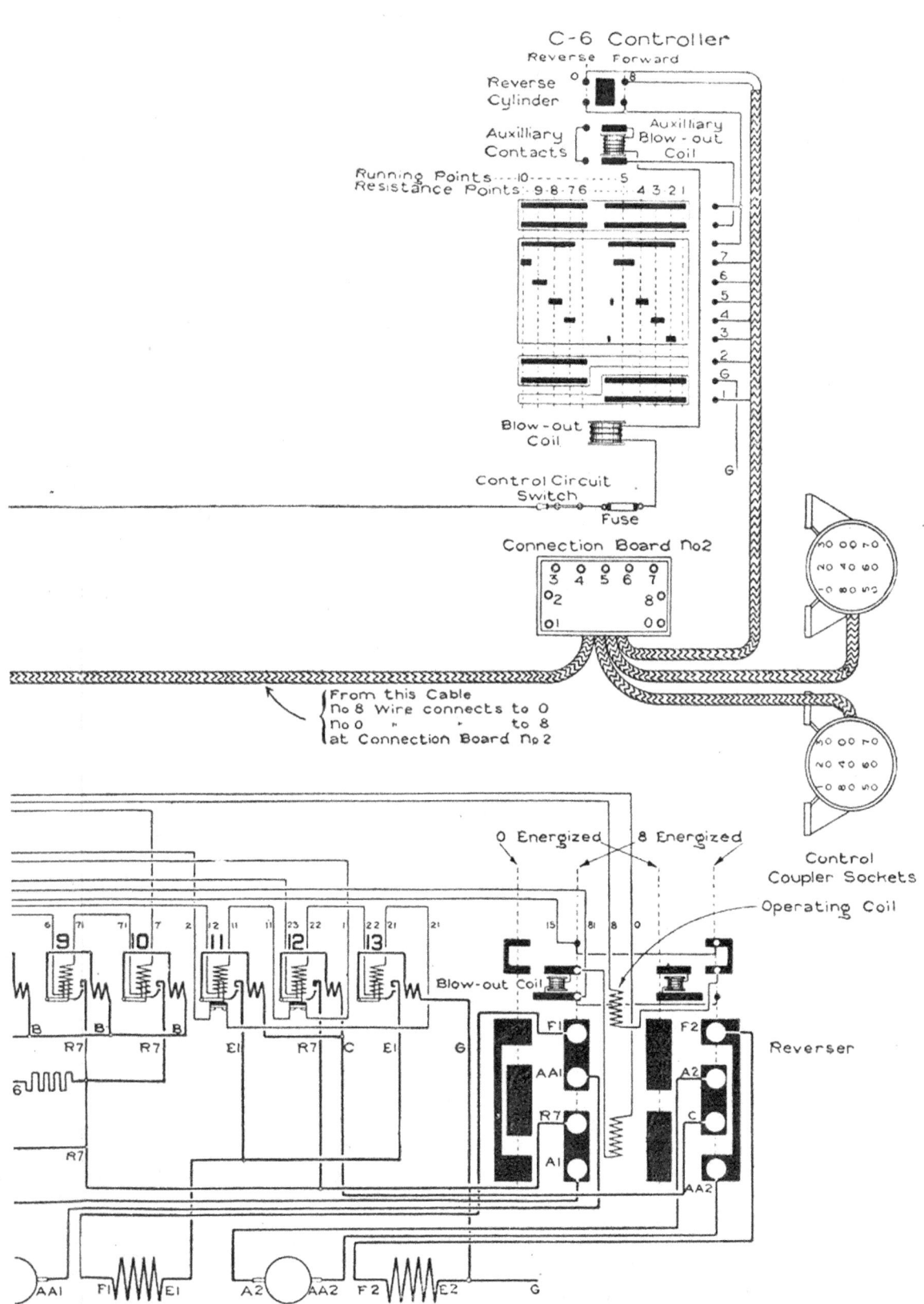

FIG. 86.

troller are 5 and 10, 5 being the series connection of the motors and 10 the parallel connection. The intermediate points are resistance points. As this system of control is made up of separate electrically operated switches these may be located in any available position and are generally placed under the car floor.

The Westinghouse multiple train control system employs compressed air to operate the controlling apparatus, electro-magnetic valves for controlling the admission of air to the various cylinders and a low voltage control circuit for actuating the electro-magnets. The essential parts of this system consist of a series parallel controller on which is mounted an operating head consisting of a number of air cylinders, a multiple control switch and two sets of storage batteries.

The controller and operating head combines a series parallel controller with an operating cylinder, a release cylinder, two reverse cylinders, a repeating switch, a limit switch, four magnetic valves and two safety switches. The operating cylinder carries two pawls on the end of its piston rod which engage two ratchet plates mounted on the end of the controller shaft and these pawls turn the controller notch by notch. The release cylinder throws the controller to the "off" position. The reverse cylinders are used to throw the reverser to "forward" or "back" and the magnet valves admit or cut off the air in the different cylinders. The repeating switch causes the controller to advance notch by notch automatically as the car is accelerating and the limit switch stops the advance of the controller when too much current is being taken by the motors The safety switch prevents the reverse switch from being thrown or the circuit breaker from being closed except when the controller is at the "off" position. All of the pistons of the air cylinders move against springs which return them to their normal positions when the air is cut off.

A multiple control switch, which is operated by the motorman, is placed on each end of each car and a train is controlled from the one on the front of the leading car. This switch only controls the low voltage battery circuits which operate the magnet valves. Two sets of batteries are used alternately, one set being charged on the lighting circuit of the car while the other set is being discharged. The battery circuits are connected from car to car by means of flexible cables coupled between the cars, and the supply of air for the controller cylinders is taken from the air-brake cylinders under the cars.

When the multiple control switch handle is moved to the right to the first notch the battery circuit is closed through a magnet switch which opens a valve admitting air to one of the cylinders and the piston in this cylinder is moved forward against its spring. The function of the spring is to open the circuit breaker. On notch 2 of the control switch the battery circuit is closed through the other magnets, one of which opens a valve to one of the reverse cylinders which the air pressure turns to the "forward" position. From the reverse cylinder the air passes through a pipe to the circuit breaker cylinder, where it closes the circuit breaker. Another magnet shuts off the air from the release cylinder and opens an exhaust from it to the atmosphere. When the control switch handle is moved to notch 3 the circuit is closed through the operating cylinder magnet, the repeating switch and the safety switch. In this position of the control switch air is admitted to the operating cylinder whose piston moves forward and turns the controller cylinder one notch by means of the pawl and ratchet wheel. When this piston reaches the end of its stroke an arm which it carries opens the repeating switch. This cuts off the supply of air from the operating cylinder and the spring moves its piston back until the arm closes the repeating switch and the piston carrying the pawl again moves forward and turns the controller to the next notch. This operation is repeated several times until the controller stands at the full series position, when it is stopped through the action of an interlocking switch. When the control switch handle is moved to notch 4 the automatic notching up of the controller proceeds until the full multiple position is reached. On throwing the control handle back to notch 1 the air is cut off from the operating cylinder and admitted to the release cylinder through the action of their respective magnets. The release cylinder piston in moving carries a rack with it which turns the controller to the "off" position by means of the pinion on its shaft. The pipe furnishes connection between the brake cylinder and the release cylinder so that the controller is automatically opened when the brakes are applied. The controller, also, cannot be thrown on until the brakes are released.

To operate the train after all connections are made ready and the air pump has compressed the air in the brake cylinder to the proper pressure, move the handle to notch 1, which admits air to the circuit breaker cylinders on each car; then advance the handle to notch 2 and let it remain there a few seconds and then move it to notch 3. When at this point the controllers on all the cars will advance step by step to the full series position. By pressing a latch in the handle and moving it to notch 4 all the controllers will advance to the full multiple position. The speed at which the controllers will advance depends upon the limit switch which is arranged to stop the action of the controller when a fixed maximum of current is taken by the motors.

The controllers may be stopped in any position by bringing back the handle to notch 2, but they should only be allowed to stand at the shunt positions but a short time. The current is cut off from the motors entirely by bringing the handle back to notch 1. In order to avoid delay in starting, the handle may be advanced to point 2 before the starting signal is given, and this allows the train to be started immediately by moving the handle to notch 3. For the general inspection and remedying of troubles on this system the reader is referred to a book of instructions published by the Westinghouse Air Brake Co.

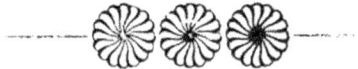

CHAPTER V.

BRAKES AND THEIR CONSTRUCTION.

The brake is a most important device for the motorman, because its purpose is to control the car when the power is cut off and cause it to slow up or stop at any desired place. The brake, when applied, consumes the energy stored in the car by the motors. This energy is overcome by the friction of the brake shoes on the car wheels. The better a motorman can estimate the distance and the less he has to use up the stored energy with the brake, the more efficient are his services, the less is the power wasted. It will be clear to apply the power up to the last moment and immediately afterwards use the brake is a wasteful performance, but there are conditions where such action cannot be avoided, for instance when stopping on a grade or when a motorman has to make many stops and his time for a round trip is measured closely with respect to the speed of the motor in use.

But before discussing the way to handle brakes let us look into the construction of some of the principal brakes in use. There are at present in use five kinds of brakes.

1. Hand brakes in which the power which draws the brake shoes against the wheels is supplied by the strength of the motorman, either by the winding of a chain on a staff or as on a few roads by a long lever.

2. Momentum or friction disk brakes in which the momentum of the car furnishes power to draw up the brake shoes through the medium of a friction disk or clutch placed on one axle.

3. Air brakes, in which the power drawing up the brake shoes is compressed air acting against a piston.

4. Electric brakes, in which the retarding force is the electricity generated in the motors which are connected to act as dynamos, the motors in this case being used to stop the car as well as to start it and run it.

5. Track brakes, in which shoes carried at the sides of the truck are pressed against the top of the track rails with sufficient force so that the friction between the shoes and rails stops the car.

While hand brakes are used on all electric cars, all but the smallest and lightest cars are now generally equipped with some kind of power brakes. Every truck has a brake mechanism consisting of various arrangements of rods, beams and levers by means of which the force applied to the brake handle or the brake levers is transmitted to the brake shoes so that they may be pressed hard against the wheels. Every make of trucks has its own style of brake rigging and the number of different makes is too great to permit a detailed description of them all, and as the general arrangement of all of them is more or less similar, a description of two or three different syles of hand brakes will suffice.

Figs. 87, 88 and 89 show three views of the truck equipped with hand brakes. Fig. 87 is a top view, Fig. 88 a front elevation and Fig. 89 a side elevation. The brake shoes, 5, are located close behind the car wheels 1, 2, 3 and 4, the normal distance between the brake shoes and wheels being about one-eighth of an inch. The shoes are supported by brake beams, 6, to which are fastened the brake rods, 7. The other ends of the brake rods are securely fastened to the cross beams, 8, which in turn engage at 9 with the equalizer bar. At the ends of the equalizer bar are secured the hook rods, 11, into which the brake chain is hooked. The chain,

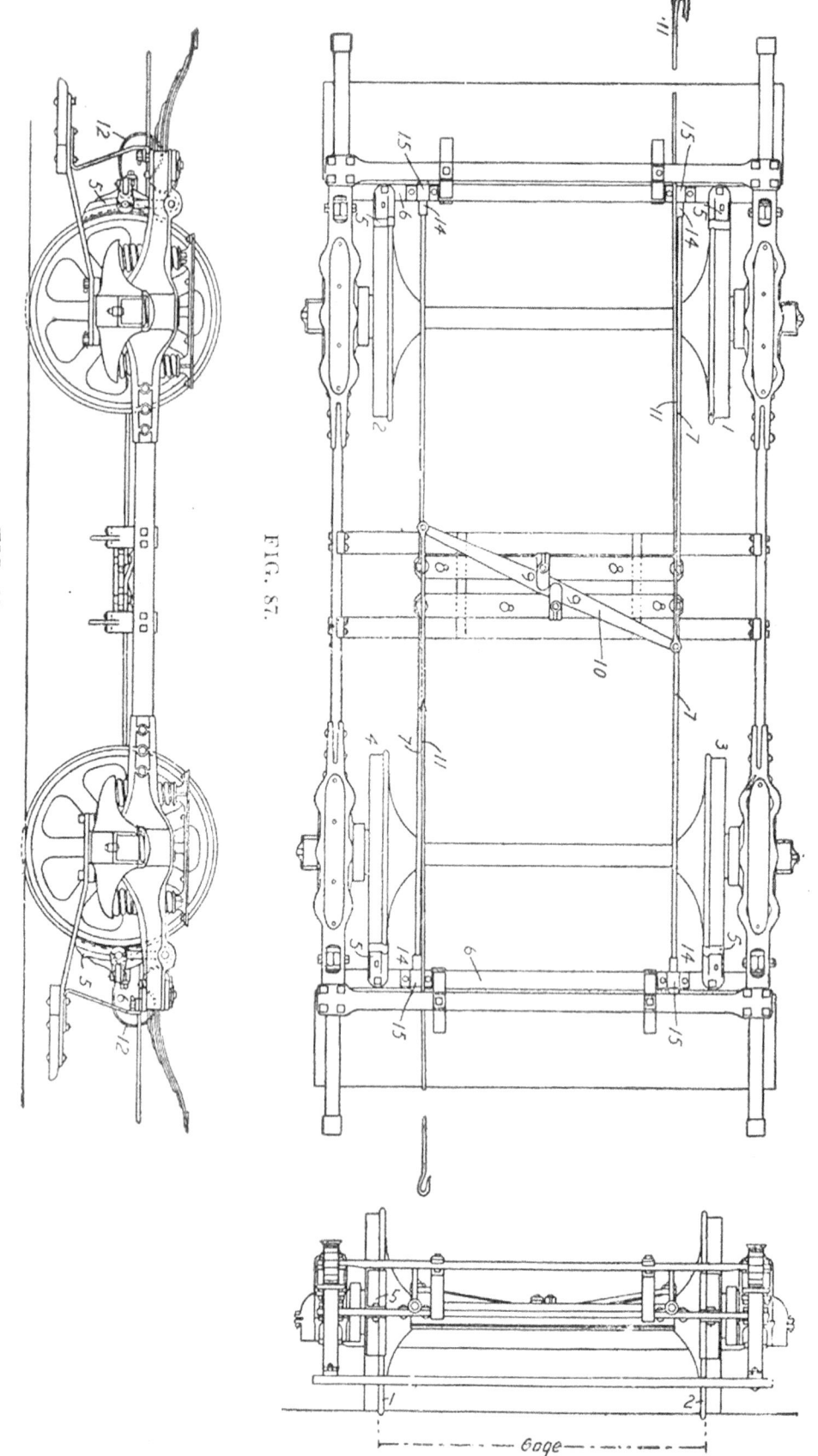

FIG. 89.

FIG. 87.

brake, staff and handle are not shown in these drawings. A heavy spring, 12, is used to remove the brake shoe from the car wheels when the brake is released. The action that takes place in braking the car is as follows:

When the motorman turns the brake handle around one or more turns he winds up the brake chain and pulls the hook rod, 11, forward and thereby moves the equalizer bar, 10, which in turn moves the cross beams, 8, 8. These cross beams in moving towards each other move rods 7, and these in turn bring the brake beams, 6, and shoes, 5, toward each other until the shoes rest firmly against the car wheels. When the brake handle is released, all the parts return to their former position. The spring, 12, assists in this latter work and helps to hold the brake shoe away from the wheel. It will be seen from this that all four brake shoes act at the same time. It is necessary to provide an adjustment in every brake, because the brake shoes wear and the slack caused by this wear must be taken up. In the truck just described this adjustment is made where the rods, 7, connect to the brake beam at points 14 near the shoes. These rods have threaded ends that screw into sleeve nuts, 15, which are held in pockets provided for them in the brake beam. A self-locking device prevents these ends from turning loose by the jolting of the car. The adjustment is made by turning the head of the nut with a wrench. The head is at the outer enclosed side of the nut, and turning it to the right, or clockwise, shortens the rod and brings the shoe nearer the wheel. The locking device does not interfere with turning the nut with a wrench, but it prevents the nut from turning due to the jolting of the car. These adjustments are placed near the brake shoes because this location enables the adjustment of each shoe separately, and consequently all the shoes may be regulated for an equal pressure on their wheels.

Fig. 90 shows another brake mechanism which is used on

the Taylor single trucks. The brake mechanism is shown in full, and the car wheels and truck are indicated in dotted lines. At the right of the illustration is seen the projecting hook rod, which is connected to lever 2. This lever is attached slightly out of center to the break beam 3, which carries the two front brake shoes, 4, 4. The equalizer rod, 5, is attached to lever, 2, by means of a link, 6. From the equalizer the rods, 7, 7, extend to the middle of the car and are connected by turn buckles, 8, 8, to the exact duplicate of the mechanism described on the other end of the car. The turn buckles have a right hand thread tapped into one end and a left hand thread in the other, so that turning them in one direction will unscrew or lengthen both rods, 7, 7, and the distance between the equalizer bars. Turning the turn buckles in the opposite direction shortens the rods, 7, 7, and consequently the distance between the equalizer bars. When these are shortened the brake shoes, 4, 4, are brought closer together. This brake is designed to secure an even pressure upon all the wheels at the same instant, even though the adjustment on both sides should not be exactly the same. If the man in charge of the cars takes up more slack on one side of the brake than on the other, the equalizer will compensate for the difference, so that each shoe bears against each wheel with the same pressure. When the brakes are idle the shoes are held a slight distance from the wheels by an adjustable release spring, 12, which can be readily adjusted so that all the shoes are an equal distance from their respective wheels. This distance is from $\frac{1}{8}$ to 3-16 of an inch, and in this position the motorman can bring the shoes against the wheels by a single turn of the brake handle. Under these conditions the speed of a car can be checked quickly, and the car is under easy control. It is hardly possible to entirely disable these brakes, as the conductor can apply the brake on the rear end of the car in case anything

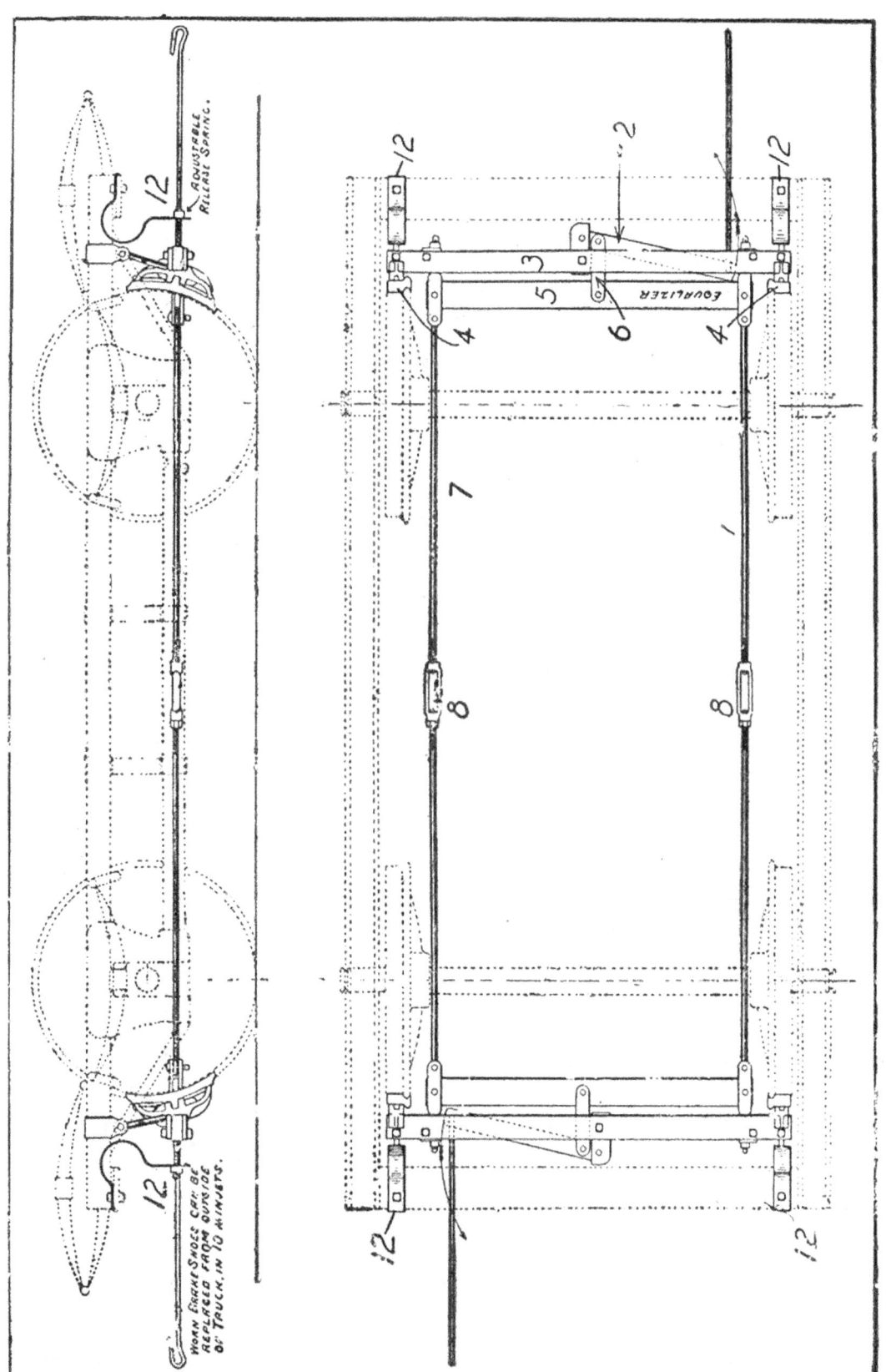

Fig. 90.

becomes disabled on the motorman's end, and if one of the brake rods and end chains give way, the brake can be operated on the opposite end.

The McGuire hand brake is shown in diagram in Fig. 91. The full truck is not shown, but simply the wheels and one side of the brake. The brake chain is attached to rod, 1, and when this rod is drawn by the brake chain attached to the brake staff, the curved lever, 2, to which it is attached, is

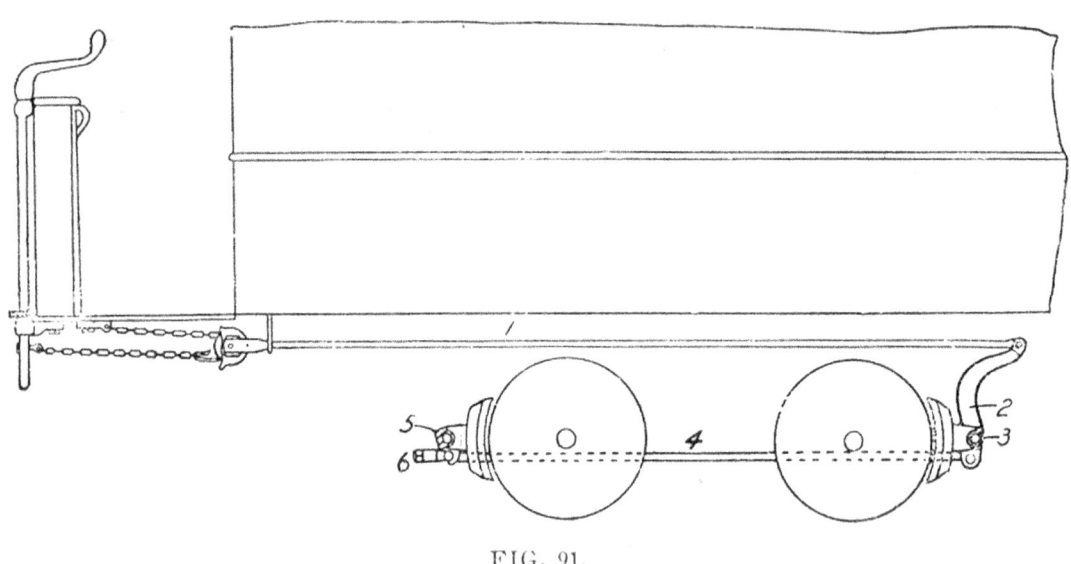

FIG. 91.

pulled over toward the left. This lever is pivoted on the brake beam, 3, and has its other end attached to rod, 4, which runs across to the other brake beam, and the rocking lever, 5. It will be seen that when the rocking lever, 2, is pulled from right to left the brake beams carrying the brake shoes are pulled together, and the shoes drawn against the wheel. To adjust the brake shoes and bring them nearer the wheels a nut, 6, is provided on the end of the rod, 4. The arrangement of the brake levers is the same on the opposite side of the truck, except that the lever, 2, is on the opposite end.

The rods on the two sides should be adjusted so there will be an even pressure on both pair of brake shoes

Fig. 92 shows the elastic brake shoe hanger of the McGuire Manufacturing Company. The spring G serves to automatically take up the wear on the pivot H, and also acts as a reactive spring to throw the shoe away from the wheels when the brake is released. The force with which these springs G act on the brakes can be regulated by the

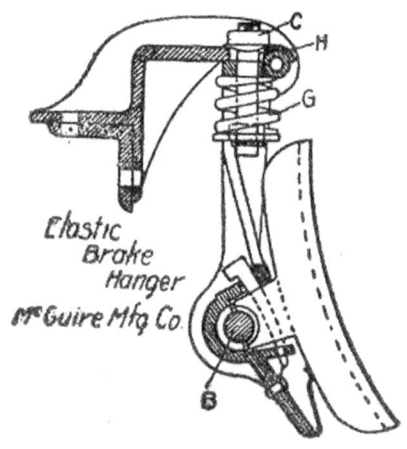

FIG. 92.

nuts C, so that the proper clearance between the shoes and the wheels can always be maintained. For instance, if the shoes on one side of the car do not stand the same distance from the wheels as on the other side when the brake is released, the nut C should be slacked off on the hanger whose shoe is farthest from the wheel, and tightened on the hanger whose shoe is nearest to the wheel. Many of the older McGuire trucks have plain standard release springs in place of the elastic hanger.

In the case of double truck cars, arrangements must be made to apply the brakes on both trucks, so that each will be operated by the motion of one brake handle. This is accomplished in various ways, generally by having either a fixed or floating lever in the center of the car between the trucks, to which the brake rods from each truck are connected. The central lever is then connected to the brake staff by means of a brake chain and rod, and by moving this rod and the central lever to which it is attached, the brakes

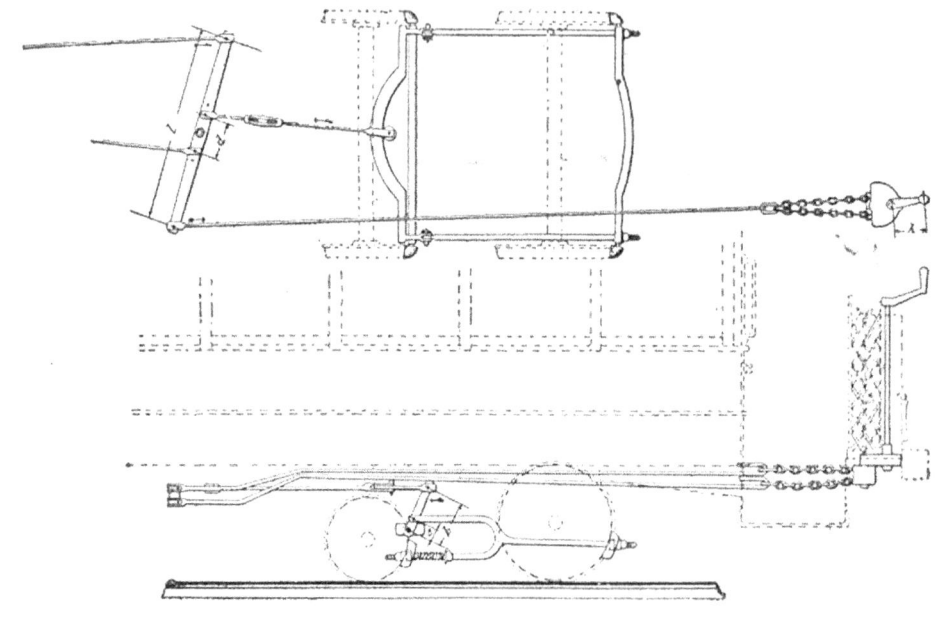

FIG. 93.

on both trucks are operated simultaneously. The arrangement of the levers of the Sterling brake for double truck cars, which is standard on the cars of the Metropolitan Street Railway, New York City, is shown in Fig. 93, and the following dimensions show the proportion of the different levers. The length of the floating lever, l, is 48 in., and the distance, d, between the pins for the arch bar rods is 9 in. The length, b, of the truck lever is 13 in. With these dimensions of levers a pull of 65 lb. at the brake handle, which is 15 in. in length, gives a total braking pressure of

29,000 lb., which is more than the weight of an empty car. The proportion of the levers recommended by the makers of these brakes is such as to make $(1 \div d) \times (b \div c) \times (h \times 85)$ equal to the total weight of the unloaded car. The chain is not coiled around the brake staff on these brakes, but there are two chains running in a double sprocket wheel which makes the operation of the brake very smooth and permits the motorman to feel even a slight touch of the brake shoe against the wheel. If the working chain breaks,

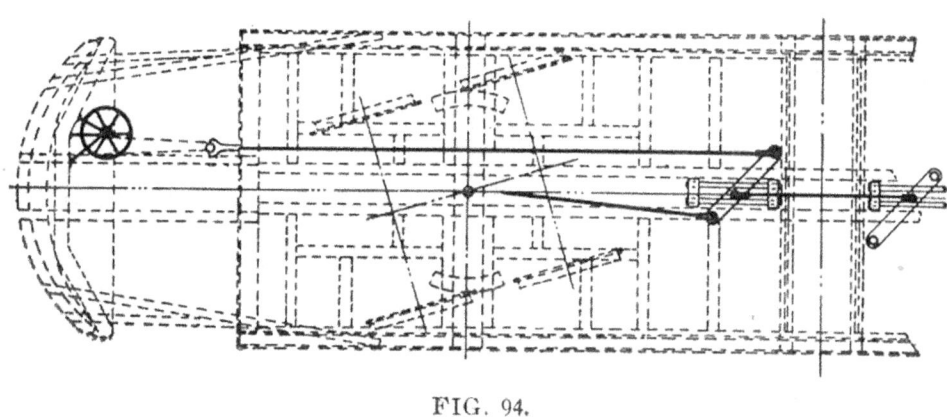

FIG. 94.

the safety chain comes into operation, thus preventing the disability of the brakes from this cause.

The standard equalizer brake rigging for double truck cars used by the Brill Co. is shown in Fig. 94. The two central equalizer levers are connected at their fulcrums by a short rod, one end of each lever is connected by a rod and chain to the brake staff, and the other end of each lever is connected by another rod to the brake rigging. The object of these brake mechanisms for double trucks is to provide a means for bringing an approximately equal pressure on all of the car wheels which is necessary in order to secure the maximum braking effect, and also to prevent one set of wheels being locked more firmly than the others, which would cause them to slide along the track without revolving, and produce flat spots on the wheels.

The Price momentum brake has a friction clutch on one axle, from which power is derived to draw up the brake chain which operates the ordinary brake rigging. In other words, the friction clutch supplies the power which is furnished by the muscles of the motorman when the common hand brake is used. With the Price brake the motorman simply pulls a lever, which forces the friction clutch to act

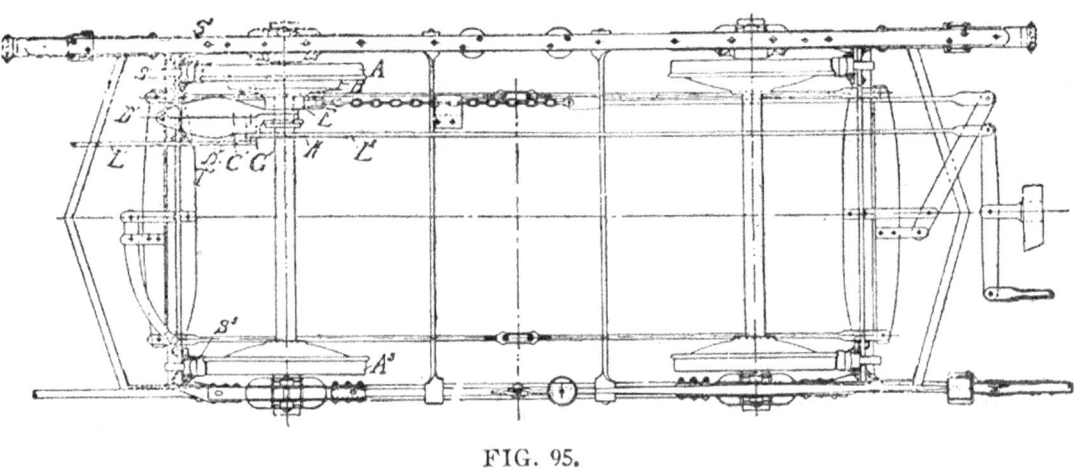

FIG. 95.

and draw up the brakes. The plan of a truck equipped with the Price brake is shown in Fig. 95. The car wheel, a, has a disc wheel, b, which may be fastened to it, or as ordinarily used, is cast on the wheel. Against this is a corresponding loose disc, e, located upon the axle. This loose disc is preferably made in two parts so that it can be easily removed, and the halves are bolted together around the axle. It is supported on brass bearings and is provided with an extended sleeve to which is attached one end of the chain, the opposite end being secured to the center lever of a double truck car, or to one of the brake levers when a single truck is used. In the early Price brakes the loose disc is pressed against the car wheel disc by a system of levers controlled by the motorman, and this causes the disc, e, to attempt to revolve with the car wheel. This movement of the disc, e, winds up the brake chain attached to it, and applies the brake. In the modern Price brakes improvemnts have been made in the method of applying the power. A hydraulic pressure pump has been added in combination with a hydraulic clutch for operating the brake. The pressure pump is located on the floor of the car platform, and is operated by means of a vertical staff, to the upper end of which a ratchet wheel is attached. The movement of this handle drives the plunger into the barrel of the pump and makes it possible to put the desired pressure upon the liquid which it contains. A pipe connects this pump with the cylinders of a hydraulic clutch that is located on the axle and operates the disc. In order to make a gradual application of the friction disc to the wheel an air pump is provided in the connections, which serves as a cushion and permits the motorman to apply the brakes as rapidly or as slowly as required This brake has an operating lever, which is located close to the dash between the hand brake staff and the motor controller. To apply the brake, pull the lever slowly for an easy stop and quickly for an emergency stop, and ease off the pull on the lever slightly just before the car comes to a stop, same as is done with the hand brake.

When going up a grade do not ease off the pull entirely, but hold the brake on till ready to start the car again. If the brake is released on a grade the car will run backwards, but can be brought to a stop by applying the brake, same as when the car is running down the grade.

The lever is provided with a ratchet and pawl, but these should not be used until after the car comes to a stop and when it is desired to hold the brake on.

Before leaving the car platform always set the hand brake.

Air brakes are now very generally used on heavy electric cars, and are principally of two kinds, known as the straight air and the automatic air brake. The "straight" air brake is the more common on electric cars, however, and is also

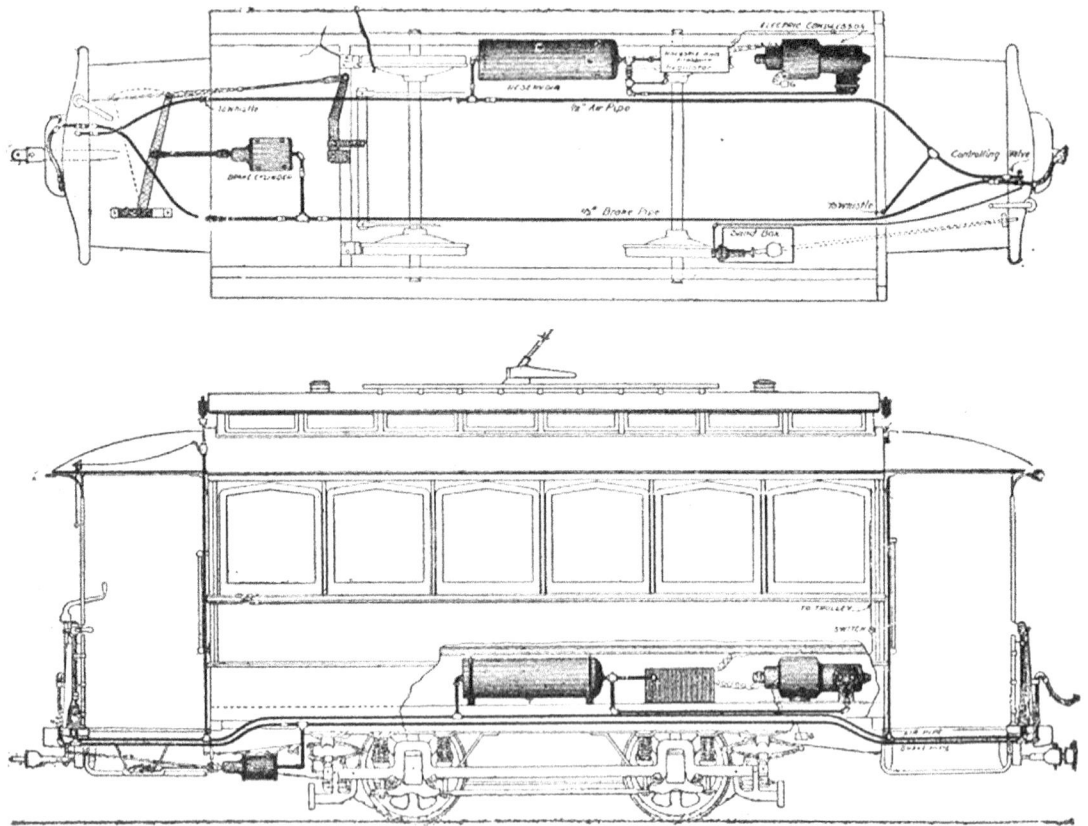

FIGS. 96 AND 97.

more simple, as we will describe the "straight" air brake first, taking as an example the Standard Air Brake Company's apparatus. Fig. 97 shows a side view of a car piped for Standard air brakes and Fig. 96 the plan of the piping as it would look from above. The air is pumped by the electric compressor under the seat into the reservoir. The compressor is simply an air pump driven by an electric motor. In some cases the pump is constantly driven from the car axle instead of a motor. The air pump is connected with the reservoir where the air is kept constantly stored under a pressure of from 30 to 40 pounds per square inch. Automatic regulators shut off the electric pump motor when the pressure reaches 40 pounds, or if the compressor is driven from the axle the pump is made to exhaust into the open air when the pressure rises to that amount. From the reservoir, pipes run to the motorman's valves on each platform and pipes also connect the motorman's valves with the brake cylinder. The brake cylinder has a piston which is connected to the brake shoe rig of the truck. To apply the brakes the motorman's valve is turned so as to let the air pressure from the reservoir into the brake cylinder which pushes out the piston and applies the brakes. To release brakes the valve is turned so as to let the air escape from the brake pipe and close the way from the reservoir to the brake pipe. If a trailer is used its brake pipe is connected to that of the motor car, so that the pressure let into the motor car brake cylinder also goes to the trailer brake cylinder.

The handle of the motorman's valve should always be on release position, that is to the extreme right, when the car is running. Between the position of "application" and "release" there is the position of lap. When making a service stop the handle should be moved to the left until it is slightly to the left of lap and immediately back to the lap position. This will admit some air pressure to the brake cylinder. The suddenness of the stop depends on the distance the handle is moved past "lap" and the length of time it is left there. To make an emergency stop immediately throw handle over as far to the left as possible and keep it there. This lets the full pressure into the brake cylinder. On slippery track some judgment must be used, however, in making an emergency stop not to slide the wheels. The air brake, and especially the compressor, needs regular attention and oiling.

The general plan of the Christensen air brakes, which are very extensively used on electric cars, is shown in Fig. 98. The compressor consists of a self-contained enclosed air pump which is either directly attached to the car axle, being operated by an eccentric, or is driven by a separate electric motor. The suction and discharge valves are so arranged that when the maximum presure is reached the compressor stops working automatically, and does not commence compressing again until the pressure is lowered. In Fig. 99 is shown the plan of equipment for a motor car and trailer. In the motor driven air compressor equipments, the current for the motor is taken directly from the trolley and the action of the motor is governed by an automatic switch controller which operates by the variation in pressure due to the working of the compressor and the consumption of air by the brakes. Fig. 99 shows the connections for a motor car and trailer.

The engineer's valve is the part of this brake mechanism which most directly concerns the motorman, and he should become familiar with its operation in the various positions shown in Fig. 100. The position for releasing is the position in which the handle should stand while the car is running. In this position there is direct communication from brake cylinder to atmosphere, consequently the shoes are kept away from the wheels by the heel springs. Don't run the car with the valve handle in lap position. It should be at slow release, or between that and quick release. In lap or center position all the ports are closed, and it will be observed that this is the only position in which the handle can be removed from the valve when changing from one end of the car to the other. If this change happens to be on a grade, the brakes are simply set, the valves put in lap posi-

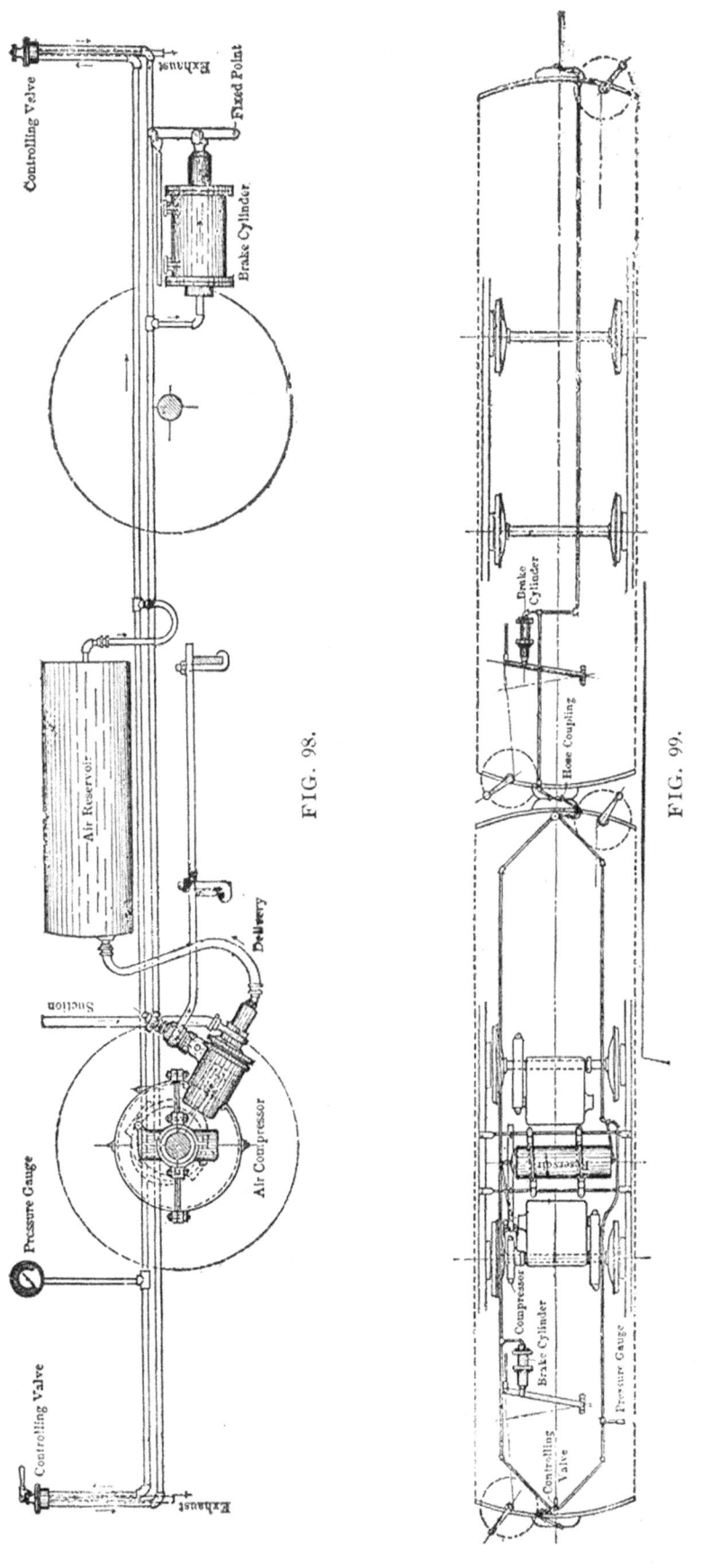

FIG. 98.

FIG. 99.

tion, and the handle removed, then the brake is released from the other end. At the emergency position a free passage is open for the air to enter the brake cylinders, applying the brake instantly with full force, and this should only be used

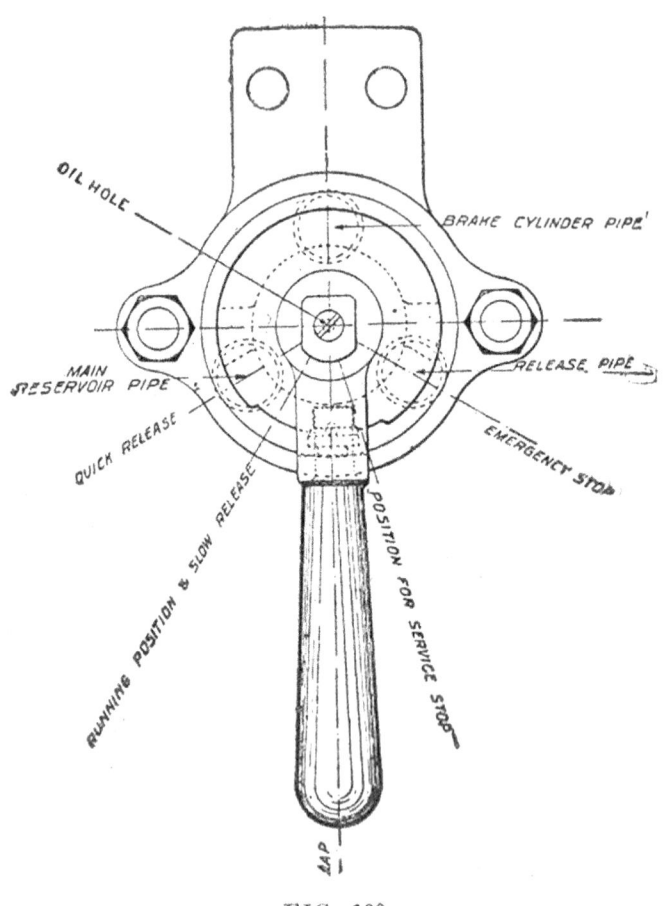

FIG. 100.

in case of necessity. The general instructions for the operation of the Christensen straight air brake are as follows:

1. To start the compressor close the canopy switch. This will automatically close the governor, so that current will pass from trolley to ground through the motor, thus driving the compressor.

2. Should the compressor refuse to work under this con-

dition, the fuse may be blown. If so, do not put in a heavier fuse than specified for the size of the compressor. If the fuse is in order, you should try to locate the trouble if you can readily do so; if not, you should report the matter to the proper person.

3. All the stop-cocks on the train pipe, except on the front and rear ends of the train, should be open. When open, the handle stands crosswise to the pipe and when closed it stands parallel with it.

4. To cut out a standard governor close the ¼-inch stop-cock so that the T handle stands crossways with the pipe; then move the governor plunger so as to make contact and thus close the circuit. The compressor can now be started and stopped by the hand switch in the canopy, but you should not forget to start and stop the compressor to keep the pressures within the desired limits of 70 pounds minimum and 80 to 90 pounds maximum.

Lap Position.—The engineer's valve is made with a detachable handle, which is only removable in what is known as lap position, in which position the valve is neutral in the same manner as the main controller is by removing the reverse handle.

Service application of the brakes is effected by moving the handle of the engineer's valve to the first notch on the right. As soon as a sufficiently hard pressure is brought against the wheels, the handle may be moved back into lap position, whereby the brakes remain set at that pressure. If it is desired to set the brakes a little harder, repeat the operation. By moving back to lap without releasing, the handle may be removed and the brake released from the other end of the car; this feature is very valuable, especially where the terminus is on a grade.

Slow Release of the Brakes.—By moving the handle from lap position to the first notch on the left a slow release of the brakes is effected, which release may be checked in the same way by moving the handle back to lap position, the same as in service application of the brakes.

Emergency Application.—This is effected by moving the handle from lap as far as it will go to the right, in which position a large passage is afforded to allow compressed air to travel from the main reservoir to the brake cylinder and the application of the brakes is practically instantaneous. The emergency application should not be made except when absolutely necessary.

Quick Release.—By moving the handle from lap position to the left as far as it will go, a quick release is effected in the same manner as a quick application, by establishing a large opening from the brake cylinder to the atmosphere, whereby the pressure escapes quickly from the brake cylinder, thereby letting off the brakes in a very short space of time.

Running Position.—When the brakes are not being applied or released, the handle of the engineer's valve should always be on the first notch to the left, or that of slow release.

Brake Leverage.—The leverage and total pressure on the brake cylinder is so proportioned that under ordinary circumstances, with a dry rail, the wheels cannot skid. If the rail is in bad condition for stopping, the leverage and pressure being the same as under normal conditions, would probably skid the wheels if the brake cylinder be charged with the full pressure.

In such instances care should be taken not to slide the wheels, by not introducing too much pressure to the brake cylinder. If the wheels slide, which can be instantly felt, the handle is moved over to slow release, letting out air until the wheels again revolve, then back to lap, and release again just before the car comes to a dead stop, to prevent the disagreeable jar which follows if a car comes to a dead stop with the brakes applied.

The Westinghouse air brake is the one in general use on steam roads. With it the pressure is kept constantly on the train pipe from one end of a train to the other. A reduction of this pressure causes an application of the brakes so that letting air out of the train pipe, either by the motorman's handle or by the breaking of a hose, will set the brakes. To explain properly the action and mechanism of these brakes would take more space than is allowable in this book, and we would refer any motorman handling these brakes to the instruction books issued by the Westinghouse Air Brake Company.

The General Electric Company's electric brake, which is in use on a number of cars, has as its fundamental principle the utilizing of the live energy stored in the moving car to generate an elctric current in the motors independent from the power-house current, and the use of this current to bring the car to a standstill. It is produced in the motors which are connected to act as dynamos. It stops the car partly by its retarding effect on the motors themselves and partly by a magnetic disc mounted on each axle. The controllers used with the General Electric Company's electric brake are of the B type. The action is as follows: Suppose a car provided with an electric brake is to be brought to a stop. The motorman first brings his controller to the "off" position and thereby disconnects the car from the line and power house; then by moving the handle around to the left of "off" position to the special brake notches, the armature connections are reversed and the motors are connected to form a closed circuit through a resistance and the brake disc magnets, as shown in Fig. 101. The motors running with the circuit closed in this way act as dynamos and generate current. This current tends to stop the motors and also to cause the magnetic clutch on the axle to act and aid in stopping the car.

To operate an electric brake requires a little practice on the part of the motorman, but when the principle is clear it is an easy matter. It should first be understood that the amount of current generated in the motors, and consequently the braking effect, depends on the speed at which the motors are running, and that if the brakes are to take

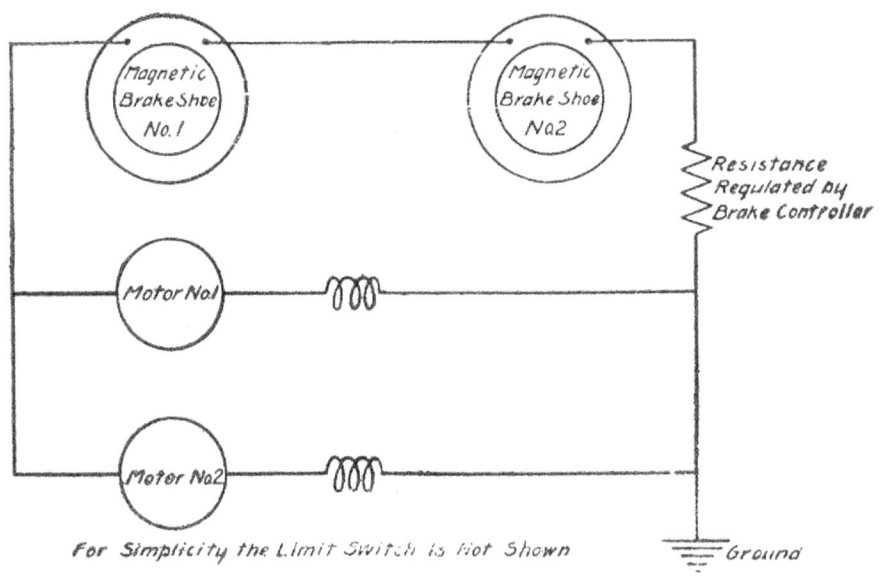

For Simplicity the Limit Switch is Not Shown

FIG. 101.

hold evenly from the beginning to end of a stop the resistance which is in the brake circuit must be steadily cut out. For example, when it is desired to stop when running at full speed, the controller handle is moved to the first brake point. The motors start generating current to retard the car, but as the car slows down a little this current begins to die out, and the handle should be promptly moved onto the next point to cut out some more of the resistance from the brake circuit and allow more current to flow, and so on until the car is stopped. The motorman should promptly advance the handle from one point to the next of the brake controller as fast as he feels the current failing on a point. The quickness of the stop will depend on the rapidity with which the handle is moved from point to point, and in emergencies it may be found necessary to move two or more points at a time. There is never need to reverse on a car having an electric brake, as the brake will stop as quick or quicker than reversing and is not so hard on the machinery. On grades it is necessary to use the hand brake to hold the car while stopping, for the electric brake lets go as soon as the car stops.

The electric brake on the Walker type S controller is described in the foregoing chapter on controllers.

The Murrey anti-friction brake has a cast iron collar keyed to the car axle next to the wheel and also a brass sleeve. Around the sleeve is a drum which is free to rotate and around which the brake chain winds. A portion of the sleeve is threaded, and the nut covering this part, which is separated from the drum by ball bearings, has a lever projection. Two levers connect to the car platform, and by forcing them forward the drum is set against the revolving collar and the friction causes the drum to revolve, winding the chain and setting the brake. The ball bearings enable any pressure to be maintained and render it impossible for the brake to set.

The Magann air brake system uses compressed air which is stord in tanks, but is not compressed upon the car as in the air brakes previously described. At the car barn or other central point a storage tank is provided containing compressed air at about 30 pounds pressure per square inch, and the tanks on the car are filled from this storage tank in a few moments. A sufficient tank capacity is provided to be sufficient for from 300 to 500 stops, or several round trips over an ordinary city route. The initial pressure in the main reservoir on the car is usually 300 pounds per square inch; by a reducing valve this is lowered to 50 pounds or less, according to the speed and weight of the cars, at which pressure the air enters the auxiliary reservoirs on the cars. From the auxiliary reservoir to the brake cylinder the air is controlled by the engineer's valve. The brake cylinder is provided with two pistons adapted to be pressed towards each other through the agency of a spring, or other similar means; means are provided by the motorman's valve for connecting the air supply or reservoir to the space between the pistons whereby the pistons may be separated against the tension of the spring to apply the brake when it is desired.

To release the brake a controlling valve is operated to cut off the space between the pistons from the air supply reservoir, and to connect it with the air space of the cylinder behind the pistons whereby the pressure on the opposite side of the piston is equalized and the springs permitted to return to their normal positions.

By this arrangement of exhaust, fresh air is always supplied behind the pistons, thereby overcoming the danger of accumulating dust in the cylinder, and by connecting the compressed air between the pistons with the cylinder behind the pistons when releasing the brakes, the pressure on both sides of the piston is rapidly equalized and the springs at once force the pistons together.

The Magann storage air brakes are operated in practically the same way as other straight air brakes. To start the car, turn the handle to the right until the shoes are felt gripping the wheels and then place the valve on lap position. The lap position is the one at which the handle can be put on and taken off from the valve. If the car does not stop as quickly as desired, turn the handle to the right again until the shoes grip the wheels more firmly. The operation can be repeated again if necessary. Turning the handle to the left allows the air in the brake cylinders to exhaust and throws off the brakes. Just before coming to a dead stop the handle should be turned to the left so as to allow most of the air in the brake cylinder to exhaust.

The Westinghouse magnetic brake consists of a combination of a track brake with the ordinary wheel brake. The track brake shoe is placed between the two pairs of wheels and instead of being forced upon the wheels through an ef-

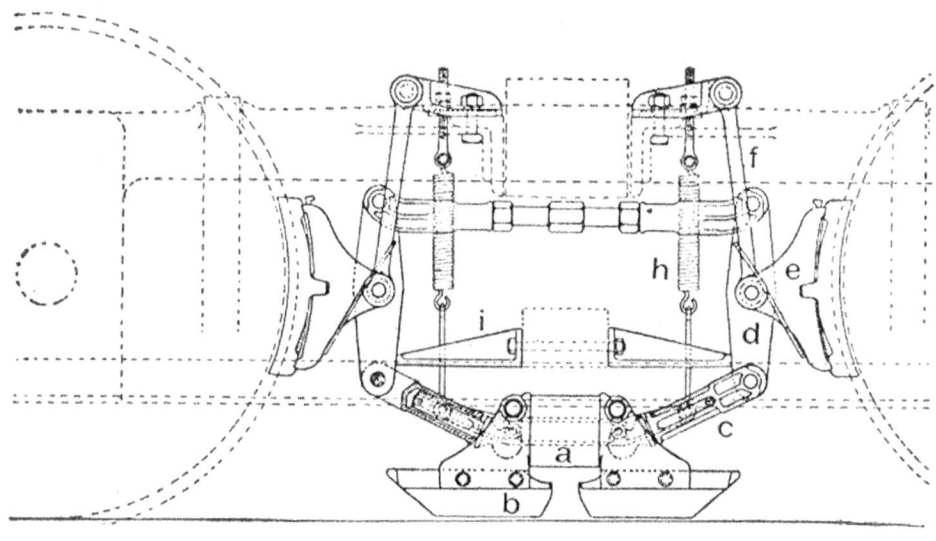

FIG. 102.

fort of the car, is drawn to the rails by an electro-magnet suspended from the car. This not only adds the track brake friction to the wheel friction for stopping the car, but there is an increase in the wheel pressure on the rails due to magnetic action. The construction of this brake is shown in Fig. 102, in which the parts of the truck are in dotted lines so as to more readily distinguish the brake apparatus. The electro-magnet, a, dividing the track brake shoe, b, into two parts, is secured by pins to the two push rods, c, and suspended at the proper distance above the rails by the adjustable springs, h. The push rods are secured by pins to the lower ends of the brake lever, d, which are connected at their upper ends by the adjustable rod, g, and at an intermediate point are pivoted to the brake shoe holders and the hanger links, f, suspended from the truck frame. The push rods, c, are telescopic, as shown in the sectional view of the one at the left, so that a movement of the track shoe toward the right relative to the truck frame causes the wheel brake shoe at the right to be applied to the wheel and the connection, g, to be moved to the left, thereby applying the wheel brake shoe at the left, the stop, i, preventing the lower end of the brake lever at the left from following the track brake shoe. A relative movement of the track brake shoe to the left is obviously accompanied by application of the wheel brake shoes through corresponding movement of the parts in the reverse order.

The brake-controlling device may be incorporated in the running controller or may be a separate device, placed by its side and operatively interlocked with it, so that neither can, through carelessness, be caused to interfere with the operation of the other. These controllers, type B, were described in the previous chapter. In the operation of the apparatus, the current is supplied by the motors, running in multiple as generators, and is divided between the electro-magnets and the diverter, in such ratio as to cause the track brake shoes to be drawn upon the rails with a force proportionate to the braking requirements. The frictional resistance of the rails to the motion of the track shoes causes the wheel brakes to be applied with corresponding force. Thus, to the ordinary retardation of the wheel brakes is added that of the track brake. The force of application depends upon the current and upon the electro-magnets operating the brake shoes. The attractive force of the rails upon the magnets is under the control of the motorman up to a limit of 150 lb. per sq. in. of brake shoe surface in contact with the rails.

The strength of the magnet is limited by the sectional area of the rail, acting as armature, and where the weight of the car makes a magnet of greater strength desirable, the track shoe is divided into three parts, instead of two, and wound to form a three pole magnet, or two electro-magnets with one common pole. With this brake the diverters or resistances are arranged in two sets, one inside and the other outside of the car. Those inside are used to heat the car, for which the starting current and braking current is ample. The two sets of diverters may be so combined that any desired portion of the heat generated may be used in the car and the remainder, if any, passes into the open air.

The friction of the track brake shoe may also be adjusted to some extent through the angular inclination of the push rods, c, by which some of the weight of the car may be thrown upon the track shoes, the levers d being correspondingly adjusted to reduce the wheel brake shoe pressure in proportion as the weight is transferred to the track shoe. The current declines with the speed during a stop, and in bad weather, when the condition of the rails is liable to be accompanied by wheel sliding, the braking force operating the wheel brake is correspondingly reduced so that the force of application of the wheel brakes is automatically proportioned to the rail friction which rotates the wheels. If by chance the wheels should slide upon the rails, the interruption of wheel rotation cuts off the track-magnet current, through which the pressure of the brake shoes upon the wheel is instantly relaxed and rotation of the wheels is resumed, without injury or serious loss of time.

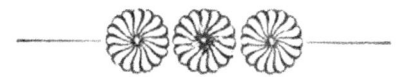

CHAPTER VI.

ELECTRIC TRACTION SYSTEMS.

We are familiar with the trolley car running alone or with a trailer, and taking current from an overhead trolley line; but in addition to this there are several other methods by which cars are operated by electricity. The overhead trolley is probably the cheapest of any electrical system to build, and is easily maintained and operated, but beside this there are third rail, conduit, surface contact and storage battery systems, and systems using two or more overhead trolley wires and electric locomotives.

THIRD RAIL SYSTEM.

The third rail system is one in which a rail called the third rail is substituted for the overhead trolley. The third rail may be placed either between the two track rail or outside of them. The third rail system is at the present time assuming considerable importance in the electric railway field, and this type of construction is required where heavy cars are made up into trains and operated at high speed. The reason that the third rail system is preferable to the overhead trolley in such cases is that the weight and speed of trains requires an amount of current which is too great to be collected by the overhead trolley wheels owing to its very limited contact. In the third rail system the sliding contact is maintained by means of a shoe which slides along the top of the third rail, and may be given sufficient area to carry any required amount of current. The first commercial installation of the third rail system was on the intra-mural railway at the World's Fair in 1893. It was next adopted by the elevated roads of Chicago and afterwards on a branch line of the New York & New Haven railroad. The system was subsequently extended to various branches of the same road. It was next used on the Albany & Hudson Ry., after which it was installed on the Aurora, Elgin & Chicago Ry. A third rail system in which the third rail is protected by a wooden sheathing on top and at one side has been installed on the Wilkesbarre & Hazelton railroad. All the elevated roads in Chicago, Boston and New York are now equipped with the third rail system. The third rail is elevated about six inches above the level of the track rails and is supported on insulators resting on the ties. In this country the third rail is always located outside of the track rails, the general practice being in elevated railway work to locate the third rail 20 inches from the track rail, and in surface road work 27 inches from the track rail. In the earlier third rail systems, insulators were made of wood, but it has been found that after a year or two of service the wood absorbs sufficient moisture to partly short circuit the insulator, and cause considerable loss through leakage. A number of these wooden insulators have been found burning at various times, and it has been noticed that the burning takes place at the inside of the insulator instead of at its surface, showing it to be due to capillary action of the water lying upon the ties and road bed. Aside from the location of the supply conductor, there is no difference between the third rail and the overhead system, so far as the circuits upon the car are concerned. The current from the third rail is collected by means of a shoe which slides along the top of the rail. The shoe is fastened to the journal box or some part of the truck by means of a hinged joint which allows it to bear on the rail with a pressure equal to its weight. It is, of course, thoroughly insulated from all metallic parts of the car.

The third rail system is applicable only to roads running upon a private right of way and is especially adapted to the operations of cars in trains, which requires a larger amount of current than can be collected by one trolley wheel. Shoes are placed at the journal boxes of all the cars so that on a long train the current is collected at a number of different points. Where the road crosses a highway the third rail is broken, stopping at each side of the crossing, and the car is allowed to drift over the gap without current. The continuity of the third rail circuit is secured by attaching an underground cable between the two ends of the third rail, and these ends are built with a downward curve so that the shoes, which can only drop slightly below their normal position, do not make violent contact with the rail, but ride up on the curved portion.

SURFACE CONTACT SYSTEMS.

Surface contact systems are those in which there are no exposed conductors, and a number of such systems have ben devised chiefly to avoid the use of overhead wires or open underground conduits. While these systems vary considerably as to details they all contain similar essential parts. These are contact plates or buttons of iron set at short intervals apart between the tracks, collector bars carried under the cars which make contact with the buttons, and a feeder cable buried in the ground which is connected to each button by means of a magnetic switch. Normally there is no current in the buttons and they are "dead" except when a car is directly over them, but when the collector bar comes in contact with a button it is magnetized and this magnetism closes the magnetic switch and completes the circuit from the underground conductor through the button thence to the collector bar and to the car circuits. The buttons are placed close enough together so that before the collector bar has left one button it makes connection with the next one. Sometimes two rows of buttons are used and two bars under the car, one for magnetizing the switches and the other for collecting the current. The current for magnetizing the bar and buttons may be obtained from a few cells of storage battery carried on the car. This system is used to a considerable extent in Paris, France, and has just been applied to eleven miles of track in Wolverhampton, England, but has not been used in this country except on a small scale in yards and about manufacturing establishments. It is less reliable than the trolley system owing to the use of so many underground magnetic switches which are liable to get out of order and fail to open, thus leaving "live" contact buttons in the streets.

CONDUIT SYSTEM.

The conduit system is one in which the conductors are carried in a conduit under the surface of the street similar to a cable railway conduit. Unlike the other system described the conduit system does not make use of the tracks for a return circuit, but instead, both the positive and negative conductors are supported on insulators fastened inside of the conduit. The current is taken from these conductors by means of a trolley extending down through a slot in the surface of the road. This underground trolley is called a plow. The conductors are generally composed of copper bars and the plow contains sliding contact pieces which rest on these bars. One side of the plow collects the current, which is led to the controllers and motors, after which it passes again to the plow contact which is in connection with the return circuit.

This system is in use in New York City and Washington, D. C., and in a few European cities where overhead conductors are prohibited. It is very expensive to build, costing in the neighborhood of $100,000 per mile.

STORAGE BATTERY CARS.

A storage battery car is one which has electric current stored in cells or batteries in the car, which supply current to the car motor. Such a car can run on any railroad track and requires no wires or conductors outside of itself. The storage cell consists of plates of lead immersed in acid, and these cells are charged at the power station by putting them in circuit with a dynamo, the electric current causing chemical changes in the lead. These changes represent a certain amount of electrical energy, which is given out when the batteries are connected to the car motors. The battery merely supplies current for the car and the controllers are similar to those on trolley cars and the method of operation is the same. Storage battery cars are not very extensively used, as the cost of operation is considerably higher than that of trolley cars. This is chiefly due to the batteries, which are expensive to install and which wear out rapidly under the severe conditions of street railway work.

ELECTRIC LOCOMOTIVES.

For the purpose of moving long trains of cars, switching freight cars and other purposes where the power required is so great that the motors cannot be mounted on the trucks of ordinary cars, electric locomotives are used and current is taken from an overhead wire or a third rail, as with a trolley car. These locomotives are equipped with motors of large capacity and their frames are very heavy so as to secure sufficient adhesion to the track to pull very heavy loads. The controllers and other apparatus on electric locomotives are similar to those on cars of ordinary size, being merely larger and heavier to accommodate the larger current used.

GLOSSARY.

Ampere—The standard unit of electric current which is equivalent to the current flowing through a circuit having one ohm resistance with a pressure of one volt.

$$\text{Current} = \frac{\text{Volts}}{\text{resistance}}.$$

Armature—The part of a motor or dynamo which revolves and produces power or generates current.

Brushes—On railway generators and motors they are blocks of carbon held in brass holders with light springs to press them against the commutator, and through which the current passes to or from the commutator and armature, or from the stationary conductor of the circuit to the rotary conductors or vice versa.

Brush Holders—Devices to hold the brushes; they are adjustable so that the brushes can be lifted to prevent sparking.

Circuit Breaker—An automatic switch arranged to open whenever the current becomes greater than a certain amount and endangers the machine. It consists of a few turns of wire around an iron core which becomes a magnet of greater and greater power as the current increases until it throws open the switch or releases a catch which allows a spring to open the switch.

Commutator—A set of copper segments separated by thin strips of mica insulation in the form of a drum; through the segments covered by the positive brushes the positive current passes to the armature in a motor and from it in a dynamo.

Compound Winding—The field magnets of a railway dynamo always have two windings, through one of which, the "series," the main current passes, and through the other, the "shunt," a branch of the main current passes.

Conductors—The part of the dynamo, motor or line, or circuit through which the current flows.

Diverter—A rheostat or resistance placed in circuit with a motor to reduce the current.

Electro-Magnet—An iron or steel core around which a spool of wire is placed to carry current.

Electro-Motive Force—The voltage or volts' pressure in a circuit; e. g., the trolley circuit has an electro-motive force of 500 volts. The abbreviation is e. m. f.

Field—The part of a motor or dynamo which contains the magnets.

Fuse—A strip of metal, generally some alloy of lead, which easily melts when too great a current is flowing in the circuit. It is mounted usually on a piece of porcelain called a fuse block.

Generator—Has the same meaning as dynamo, but is commonly used to denote the large machines in the station.

Horse Power—The standard rate of work being 33,000 foot-pounds per minute. If a machine can lift 1,000 pounds 33 feet in one minute its capacity is one-horse power. The abbreviation is h. p. Electrical equivalent, h. p.= 746 watts.

Insulation—A non-conductor, as air, rubber, mica, varnish, etc., through which electricity does not readily pass.

Lightning Arresters—They are devices which offer a by-pass to lightning to prevent damage to machines when the line is carrying a discharge of lightning by conducting it to the earth.

Magnetic Blow-Out—When switches are opened or the current shut off in controllers an arc is formed, or the current passing through the air from one conductor to the other. A magnet is placed near the point where the arc is formed and draws it aside and blows it out.

Ohm—The standard of electrical resistance through which one ampere of current will flow with a pressure of one volt.

$$Ohm = \frac{volts}{current}$$

Parallel or Multiple Connection—A circuit in which the current divides and part passes through each motor, dynamo or other electrical device.

Poles or Pole Pieces—The core ends which project on the fields and conform to the shape of the armature, and geerally carry the field windings.

Resistance—An obstruction to the flow of current. All substances have some resistance, but resistance boxes or rheostats have iron wire or sometimes carbon strips for the circuit. Resistance produces heat in the circuit, and by this means the current in passing through an electric car heater makes the wires very hot.

Series Connection—When the current passes through one motor, dynamo or electrical device and thereafter into one or more devices.

Sparking—The flashing of the current which occurs at the commutator when there is poor contact, the brushes are in bad order, the commutator is dirty, or the dynamo or motor is carrying too heavy a load.

Volt—The standard of electrical pressure, or the pressure to force one ampere of current through one ohm resistance. Volts=amperes x ohms.

Watt—The rate of performance of work measured electrically; the capacity of a dynamo or motor is measured in watts and is the product of volts by amperes. A kilowatt is 1,000 watts and is equal to 1.34 h. p.

INDEX.

Accidents, precautions against	41
Ampere	28
Armature	14
Armature core	76
Arrester, Lightning	25, 53, 87
Garton	89
General Electric	91
Wurtz non-arcing	90
Blow-out, magnetic	83, 104
Brakes	13
Air	142
Brill	150
Christensen	155
Construction of	141
Electric	142, 160
Hand	141
Magann	162
McGuire	147
Momentum	141
Murray anti-friction	162
Operation of	46
Price	151
Standard Air Brake Co.	153
Sterling	149
Taylor	145
Track	142
Westinghouse magnetic track	164
Brush holder	52
Choke coil	91
Circuit breaker	25
Automatic	86
I. T. E.	87
Coil, grounded	53
Commutator	74, 77
Flashing of	57
Conductors, electrical	26
Conduit system	170
Contactors	136
Contact, rail	51

Controllers, contact fingers.. 52
    Description of 92
    General Electric 104
    Master 134
    Operation of 34
    Running points 35
    Series parallel 103
    Steel Motor Co...130
    Type B..103, 105, 117
    Type C6 134
    Type D 101
    Type K...103, 104, 105
    Type L...103, 104, 115
    Type R 104, 105, 113
    Walker 126
    Westinghouse 118
Control, type M...134
Diverter 94
Dynamo 71
    Edison 74
Economy of current 34
Electro-magnet 72
Emergencies 37
Fuse 25
    Blowing of 50, 53
    Box 84
        D. E. W. 85
        General Electric 85
        Noark 85
        Westinghouse 85
Gear, split 14
Grounds 58
Heating of motors 55
Insulators 26
Kicking coil 89
Lines of Force 65
Locomotives, electric 171
Magnet 63
Magnets, field 14, 17
Motor 14
    Box frame 21

    Parts of 81
    Principles of 63
    Railway 76
Multiple connection 97
    Field 75
    Unit Control, General Electric............................133
        Westinghouse 137
Needle, magnetic 68
Ohm's Law 28
Overhead material 29
Parallel connection 96
Power, saving of... 39
   Transmitting 26
Rail, dead 51
Reversing 38
Rheostat 39
   Burnt 53
   Thomson-Houston 92
Sand box 41
Series connection 96
   -parallel connection 98
Short circuit 53, 57
Skidding 47
Stop, emergency 37
Storage battery cars 171
Surface contact systems 169
Suspension, Motor 18
Switchboard 31
Switch, canopy 24, 83
   Cut-out 104
   Multiple control 138
Third rail system 167
Transmission, electrical 31
Trolley base 23
Troubles, How to remedy 49
Trucks 12
Volt 28
Wheel, flat 57
   Slip 41
Wiring, car 21

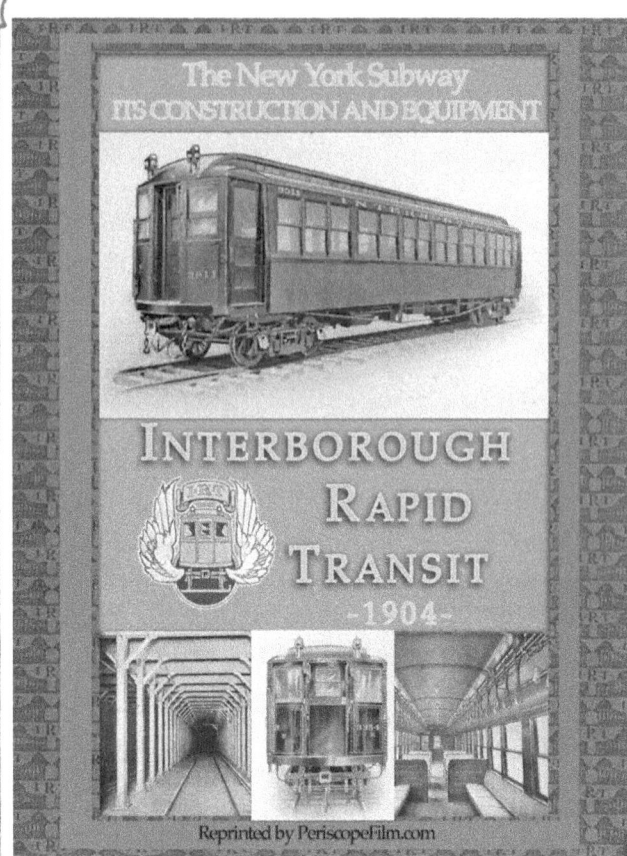

On October 27, 1904, the Interborough Rapid Transit Company opened the first subway in New York City. Running between City Hall and 145th Street at Broadway, the line was greeted with enthusiasm and, in some circles, trepidation. Created under the supervision of Chief Engineer S.L.F. Deyo, the arrival of the IRT foreshadowed the end of the "elevated" transit era on the island of Manhattan. The subway proved such a success that the IRT Co. soon achieved a monopoly on New York public transit. In 1940 the IRT and its rival the BMT were taken over by the City of New York. Today, the IRT subway lines still exist, primarily in Manhattan where they are operated as the "A Division" of the subway. Reprinted here is a special book created by the IRT, recounting the design and construction of the fledgling subway system. Originally created in 1904, it presents the IRT story with a flourish, and with numerous fascinating illustrations and rare photographs.

Originally written in the late 1900's and then periodically revised, A History of the Baldwin Locomotive Works chronicles the origins and growth of one of America's greatest industrial-era corporations. Founded in the early 1830's by Philadelphia jeweler Matthais Baldwin, the company built a huge number of steam locomotives before ceasing production in 1949. These included the 4-4-0 American type, 2-8-2 Mikado and 2-8-0 Consolidation. Hit hard by the loss of the steam engine market, Baldwin soldiered on for a brief while, producing electric and diesel engines. General Electric's dominance of the market proved too much, and Baldwin finally closed its doors in 1956. By that time over 70,500 Baldwin locomotives had been produced. This high quality reprint of the official company history dates from 1920. The book has been slightly reformatted, but care has been taken to preserve the integrity of the text.

NOW AVAILABLE AT
WWW.PERISCOPEFILM.COM

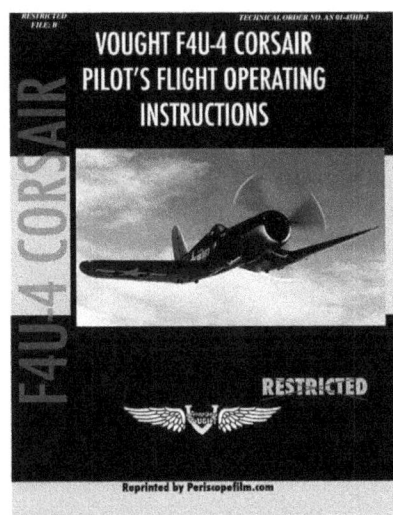
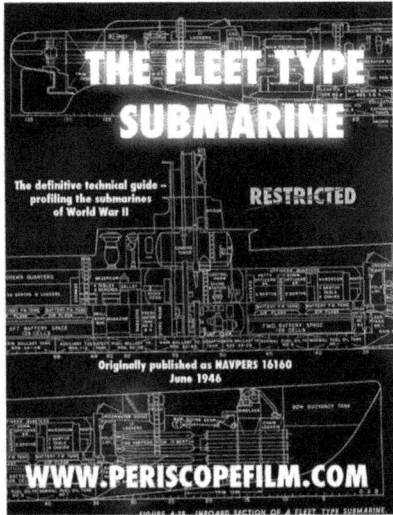

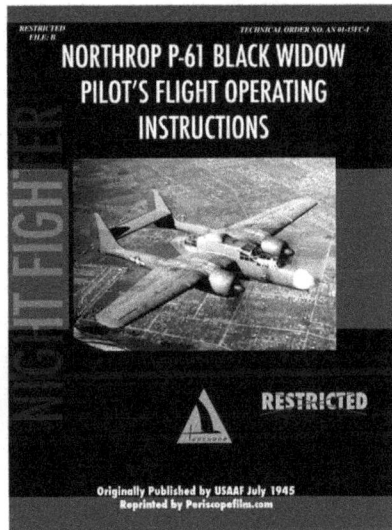

ALSO NOW AVAILABLE
FROM PERISCOPEFILM.COM

©2006-2010 PERISCOPE FILM LLC
ALL RIGHTS RESERVED
ISBN #978-1-935700-06-7
WWW.PERISCOPEFILM.COM

www.ingramcontent.com/pod-product-compliance
Lightning Source LLC
Chambersburg PA
CBHW081939170426
43202CB00018B/2946